To Grant
Happy Christmas 1989,
with Love from
Mum and Dad.

# SOUTH AFRICA
## magnificent land

# SOUTH AFRICA
# *magnificent land*

Published by The Reader's Digest Association
South Africa (Pty) Limited, Cape Town

First edition copyright © 1988
Second printing 1989
The Reader's Digest Association South Africa (Pty) Ltd,
130 Strand Street, Cape Town 8001

®  READER'S DIGEST is a registered trademark of
·The Reader's Digest Association, Inc,
of Pleasantville, New York, USA

ISBN 0 947008 45 4

*The gentle light of dawn invades the dark corners of Natal's Ndumu Game Reserve.*

# A UNIQUE PICTORIAL RECORD
# OF A TRULY MAGNIFICENT LAND

*As the eastern sky begins to blush with dawn, a single-engined Cessna rattles down a dirt airstrip to climb towards the sun. On board are a pilot and a photographer, determined to capture the magnificence of a land still bathed in the tender light of a new day.*

*The photographer is no stranger to crack-of-dawn assignments; in fact, he is regarded as South Africa's foremost aerial cameraman. This time, however, he has one of the greatest challenges of a long and exciting career: to recreate on film the awesome beauty and astonishing contrasts of a subcontinent so remarkable for its natural and scenic splendours that there are few places to equal it on earth.*

*And to make the job even more challenging, he knows that the competition is fierce. In fact, he is only one of 22 top South African photographers given the same assignment by Reader's Digest: to give us the best photographs of their lives.*

*The result is in your hands, a book that contains the very finest pictures of our magnificent land ever assembled in one volume; a land created when the world was an infant, long before the break-up of the earth's great landmasses.*

*Here, in the cradle of the seas, are brooding mountains, silent deserts, luxuriant subtropical forests, roller-coasting downlands and untamed bushveld. Bringing vibrancy to this tranquil land are vast floral kingdoms alive with colour; rivers and streams cascading to the sea; and shimmering lakes and dams nestling in the laps of shady, green valleys.*

*HOW THE BOOK IS ORGANISED  The book is divided into eleven regions covering the entire subcontinent, each beginning with a map of the area indicating the sites of the places photographed. At the end of each section we have included special pictorial portfolios — covering natural themes such as moonscapes and clouds, the sea and the sky — that weave a natural, illuminating thread throughout the book.*

*Here is South Africa as you have never seen it before.*

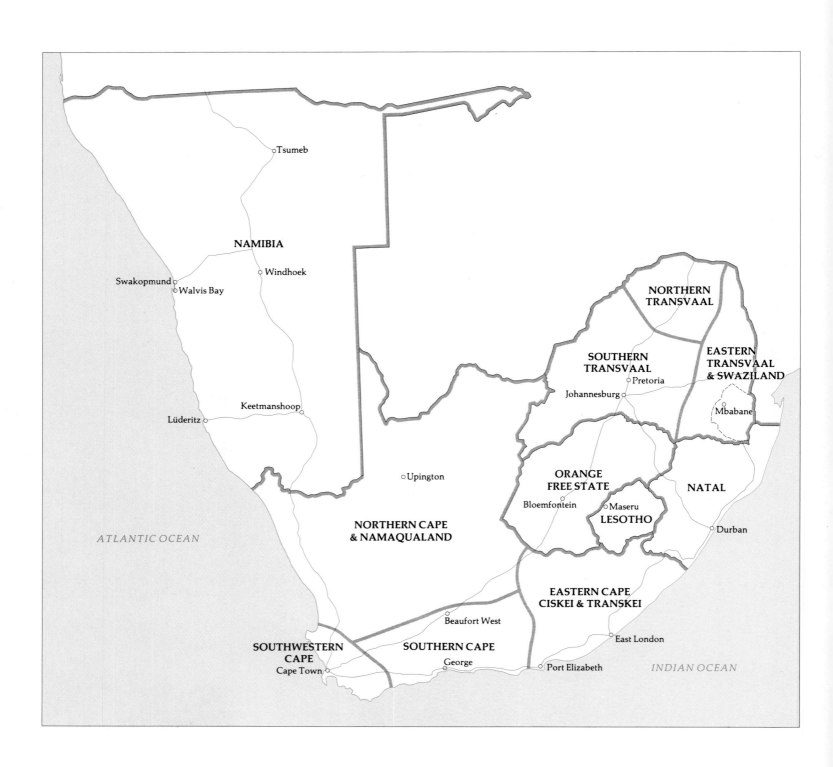

NAMIBIA

Tsumeb

Swakopmund
Walvis Bay
Windhoek

Lüderitz
Keetmanshoop

ATLANTIC OCEAN

Upington

NORTHERN CAPE
& NAMAQUALAND

NORTHERN
TRANSVAAL

SOUTHERN
TRANSVAAL
Pretoria
Johannesburg

EASTERN
TRANSVAAL
& SWAZILAND

Mbabane

ORANGE
FREE STATE
Bloemfontein
Maseru
LESOTHO

NATAL

Durban

EASTERN CAPE
CISKEI & TRANSKEI

Beaufort West
East London

SOUTHWESTERN
CAPE
Cape Town

SOUTHERN CAPE
George
Port Elizabeth

INDIAN OCEAN

# CONTENTS

*Nature's awesome giants of the Namib.*

# PARADISE AT THE END OF AFRICA

*LIKE A CROOKED FINGER snaking out into the seething wilderness of the southern ocean, the Cape of Good Hope stands in magnificent isolation on the edge of Africa. This is nature's finishing touch to a geologic masterpiece Sir Francis Drake called 'the fairest Cape in the whole circumference of the earth'.*

*It is here, beneath the sandstone countenance of Table Mountain, that nature has bestowed some of her most precious gifts: dazzling white beaches washed by the surf of two oceans; precipitous cliffs falling away from the sides of a hump-backed peninsula; a panoramic bay curving sickle-like for 30 km to the southern reaches of the Hottentots-Holland Mountains; and the world's most spectacular floral kingdom, spread across the mountains and valleys in a seemingly endless carpet of breathtaking colours.*

*This is a tranquil corner of Africa, a land of plenty where whitewashed Cape Dutch homesteads bask amongst a patchwork of vineyards, wheatfields and orchards in the temperate luxury of a Mediterranean climate. Dominating the landscape is the brooding presence of the Hex River, Du Toitskloof and Jonkershoek mountains. Their serrated peaks, once a bulwark against the oxwagons of early explorers, are now a nature lovers' paradise, where long-tailed sugarbirds and multicoloured sunbirds sample the nectar of fynbos in the company of baboons and dassies.*

*A breaker thunders shorewards.*

*The Hottentots-Holland Mountains tower above the gentle sweep of the False Bay coastline, where tranquil waters wash an unspoilt shore.*

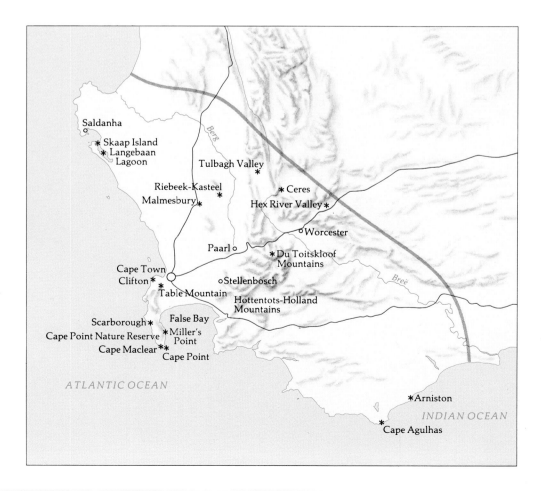

## GRAND OLD GUARDIANS OF THE BEACHES

*Battered by northwesterly storms in winter and gale-force southeasterly winds in summer, the Cape Peninsula's ancient sandstone peaks act as natural deflectors, protecting some of the world's most beautiful bays and beaches. In summer, when the southeast wind buffets the eastern flanks of Table Mountain and the Twelve Apostles, many coves and beaches on the western side remain tranquil and wind-free — ideal retreats for sunseekers and other holidaymakers. Conversely, when the northwest wind blows, the waters of False Bay on the protected eastern side are often calm, attracting beachgoers and divers to the granite shoreline.*

*The sea buffets a rocky coastal terrace at Cape Agulhas.*

*Sun-splashed beaches, beautiful bays and headlands of folded rock dominate the coastal drive between Gordon's Bay and Cape Hangklip.*

*Cool waters of the Atlantic wash ivory-coloured sands at Clifton, the favourite haunt of sun-worshippers from all over South Africa.*

## MIGHTY CURRENTS ALONG THE CAPE COAST

*Two great ocean currents influence life in the sea around the southwestern Cape shoreline. Along the west coast the nutrient-rich waters of the cold Benguela Current create a fertile environment for billions of microscopic organisms that lure massive shoals of pelagic fish such as pilchard, anchovy, mackerel and maasbanker. Along the eastern seaboard, the warm Agulhas Current plays host to a greater variety of fish which appear in smaller numbers.*

*The sea is a vast reservoir of minerals and salts that, together with sunlight, enables huge populations of phytoplankton to survive and flourish. These minerals and salts include sodium chloride, magnesium chloride, calcium sulphate, barium, arsenic, silver and gold.*

*Reflected by low-lying clouds, the crimson colours of sunset merge with dark blankets of kelp fringing the Cape shoreline.*

*Beds of kelp sparkle like black diamonds in a turquoise sea.*

*Translucent waters shimmer and swirl against a lazy shore at Miller's Point. In the background are the Hottentots-Holland Mountains.*

*A sea of dunes forms gentle corrugations on the coastline sweeping eastwards from the village of Arniston on the southwestern Cape coast.*

*A leaden sky hangs over sand dunes illuminated by the sun. These sands near Arniston conceal the bones of shipwrecked sailors.*

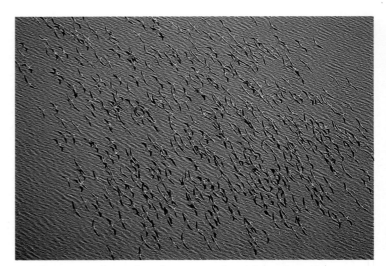

*Flamingoes fly in close formation above Langebaan Lagoon.*

*Resplendent in the sun, Skaap Island basks in the emerald waters of Langebaan Lagoon. The island is a breeding colony for kelp gulls.*

*Frustrated in their attempts to reach the tranquil waters of Langebaan Lagoon, huge Atlantic swells break up in anger on a rocky coastline.*

## RAGING FURY OFF THE CAPE OF STORMS

*The early Portuguese explorers rounding the Cape of Good Hope called it 'Cabo Tormentoso', the Cape of Storms — a cruel stretch of wind-lashed coastline that pierced their precarious route across the southern ocean. Such was the fury of the gales pounding the Cape of Storms that over the centuries the legend emerged of a sea giant named Adamastor that swallowed ships whole. Adamastor was banished to the dark, seething waters off Cape Point as a punishment for rebelling against the gods of ancient Greece; and there, so the legend goes, he remains to this day, his tormented spirit raging in the gales that batter the Peninsula.*

*Storm clouds threaten rain above the restless sea at Scarborough on the Cape Peninsula. Gale-force northwest winds batter this coastline.*

*Moody mountains near Cape Point create a brooding silhouette over a sea flattened by the gusts of the Cape's notorious southeaster.*

*Spurred on by the winds of a winter storm, icy Atlantic breakers send up an inferno of spray as they rumble shorewards at Sea Point.*

*The jagged, sun-soaked peninsula at Cape Point cuts into a dark sea.*

*Fringed with foam, the blue-green waters of the Atlantic wash a secluded beach at Cape Maclear in the Cape Point Nature Reserve.*

*Rugged peninsula at the beginning and end of Africa, the Cape of Storms pierces an ocean that stretches southwards for 5 000 kilometres.*

*Clouds reflecting the sun's rays form a radiant tablecloth on Table Mountain.*

*Table Mountain looms above green fields north of Cape Town. For centuries the mountain has served as a beacon to navigators.*

## PROUD LADY PROTECTING THE SEAS

*Like an aged matriarch and great protector, Table Mountain
stands serene and grand above the blue waters which wash the
shores of its beautiful peninsula. Covered in summer by a
mantle of swirling white cloud; obscured in winter by rolling
grey mists, the mountain reflects the moods and colours of the
changing seasons. Born as a result of intense geologic upheavals
150 million years ago, Table Mountain has become the home of
more than 2500 species of plants. Watered by streams which
cascade down its slopes in winter, fanned by the southeast wind
in summer, these plants create a lively and colourful garden on
the very doorstep of Cape Town.*

*Like a mighty bulwark against the sea, the majestic mountains of the Cape tower above the thundering surf of the Atlantic coast.*

*Southwestern Cape vines yield a rich harvest of grapes.*

*Against a backdrop of mountains, vineyards in the upper Tulbagh Valley cast long shadows in the crisp air of a summer morning.*

*Cape vines, trimmed of their foliage, bask in the winter sun.*

*Long after the harvest, autumn strikes gold into the leaves of trellised vines lying at the foot of the Du Toitskloof Mountains near Paarl.*

*Eucalyptus trees, grazing sheep and distant farmsteads are dwarfed by the roller-coasting landscape of wheatfields in the Caledon district.*

*Wheat brings a neatly contoured carpet of gold to the Cape.*

*The southwestern Cape's wheatlands are harvested in early spring, when the sun showers warmth on these rich, undulating fields.*

*Contrasting contours and colours in these farmlands near Malmesbury create a bizarre jigsaw puzzle bisected by twisting streams.*

*Mountains rear up like jagged backbones on the earth's crust, interrupting a landscape of rolling green fields near Riebeek-Kasteel.*

*Snow-capped peaks, radiant in the harsh light of the winter sun, cut rugged patterns in a pale-blue sky near the Cape town of Ceres.*

*A mantle of snow caps these ancient mountains near Ceres.*

*Streaked with snow, the precipitous flanks of the Du Toitskloof Mountains tumble down through a sea of cloud to the valley below.*

*Born in the beautiful mountains of the southwestern Cape, the Breë River gains strength as it splashes through fertile valleys to the sea.*

*Winter clouds fringe the brooding mountains of the Hex River Valley. The mountains are said to be haunted by a roaming witch.*

*Bush-covered slopes tumble down from the peaks of the Du Toitskloof into the enchanting valleys of the southwestern Cape.*

A seething wilderness of water surrounds the ragged coastline of southern Africa: two great oceans that have witnessed the first signs of terrestrial life on the planet; the break-up of its mighty landmasses; and the birth of man himself, in the cradle of the African continent.

The Atlantic Ocean, on the western edge of the subcontinent, and its icy consort, the cold Benguela Current, have spawned a parched and arid desert on the west coast; the Indian Ocean, with its warm Agulhas Current, a fringe of subtropical and evergreen lushness on the east coast. These two great oceans not only stir the atmosphere and dictate the climate of the subcontinent, they intimately affect the lives of millions of organisms, large and small — from the African elephant, feeding on the well-watered grasslands of the eastern Transvaal, to the tiniest plankton caught in the surge of a submarine current.

Hurtling forward like an ocean chariot, a breaking wave sends spume flying in its rush to the rocks of the Tsitsikamma coastline.

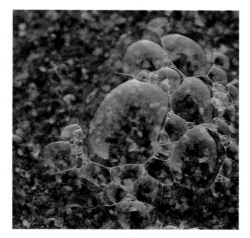

*Beach bubbles reflect sea and sky.*

*Peering out silently over a misty sea, these limpet-covered islands of rock on Natal's north coast conjure up primeval images.*

*Treacherous rollers pound Namibia's desert coast — a graveyard for ships and men.*

*Sparkling in the early morning sun, icy Atlantic waves cruise shorewards on the coastline of the Langebaan National Park.*

*Snow-white mantles of surf trail thunderous breakers near Langebaan National Park. The park is home for thousands of seabirds.*

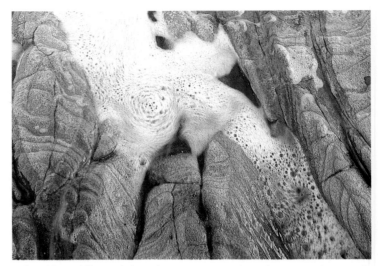

*The ebb and flow of the tide create symmetrical patterns in a pool.*

*Fog brings a ghostly pallor to a beach on the southern Cape coast.*

*Languid waters wash copper sands on Natal's north coast.*

*A tranquil shore fringes the vast expanse of the Indian Ocean. Beneath the placid sands is an unseen world teeming with tiny creatures.*

# PARADISE BETWEEN PLAINS AND SEA

*THE GRACEFUL, SINUOUS CURVES of the southern Cape coast embrace a hinterland of astonishing beauty, known to the early Khoikhoi as 'man laden with honey' — or Land of the Outeniqua.*

*Nestling between the peaks of the Outeniqua and Langkloof mountains in the north, and the translucent waters of the Indian Ocean in the south, this narrow coastal terrace nurtures a forested kingdom of staggering proportions. Here gigantic yellowwood trees break through a roller-coasting canopy of green which stretches as far as the eye can see. In this dim, green, creeper-draped world, elephants pad about the forest floor in the company of bushpigs, vervet monkeys, bushbuck and blue duiker, while the luxuriant foliage camouflages a richly diverse population of birds and insects. This is the heart of the Garden Route, where rivers of black water slash through deep-gorged mountains to the roaring waves of the Indian Ocean and the submarine brilliance of its depths; where tiny settlements, with evocative names, such as Tsitsikamma, Wilderness, Storms River and Nature's Valley reveal romantic, rocky coves, lazy rivers and sun-splashed beaches.*

*Inland, freshwater lakes, separated by huge sand dunes from the sea, provide a haven for water birds, fishes and man. Further north, where the ribs of the Swartberge pierce the pale-blue sky, a panorama unfolds of vast plains stretching to hidden horizons. This is the Great Karoo, burial ground of dinosaurs; home of isolated farmsteads; a region so climatically estranged from the great forests, flower-covered mountains and cool sea, that it could be part of another continent.*

*A tranquil river winds through a forested valley near Plettenberg Bay. Rivers like these cut through magnificent mountain scenery on their way to the coast.*

*Leaves in the Tsitsikamma forest.*

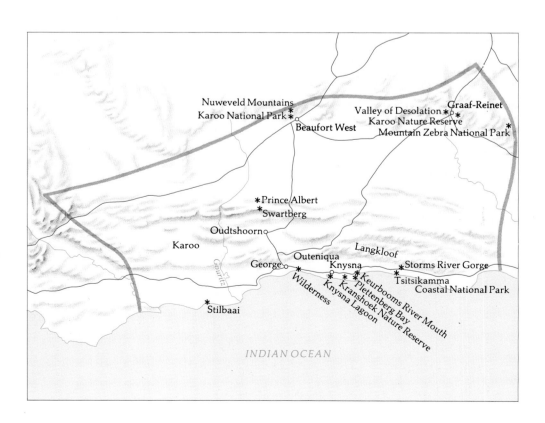

*Deep within the tranquil recesses of the Tsitsikamma forest, a stream splashes through a world of creeper-draped trees on its journey to the sea.*

*Framed by precipitous walls of rock, the Kaaimans River tumbles into a dark pool near Wilderness. These waters are reputed to be haunted.*

*The Indian Ocean's raging surf pounds the rocky shoreline of the Tsitsikamma Coastal National Park, a nature lover's paradise.*

*Early morning mist accentuates the brooding beauty of the formidable Storms River gorge near the river's confluence with the sea.*

*Indigenous forest and fynbos clothe the mountains in the Kranshoek Nature Reserve, high above the blue waters of the Indian Ocean.*

*Massive cliffs, their sides battered and broken by erosion over the years, tumble into the seething waters of the Indian Ocean near Knysna.*

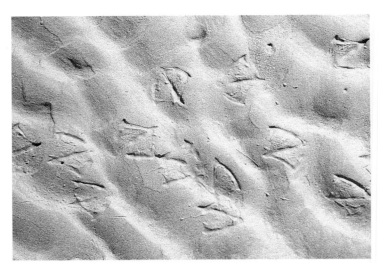

*Webbed feet create strange patterns in rippled sands at Knysna.*

*The Keurbooms River meets the Indian Ocean in a torrent of rushing water. The river was named after trees along its banks.*

*The warm, translucent waters of the Indian Ocean wash the sands of a deserted beach near Knysna on the southern Cape coast.*

*Huge swells sweeping in from a turbulent sea break against jagged rocks on the southern Cape coast, sending spray swirling skyward.*

## COASTAL WONDERLAND OF THE SOUTHERN CAPE

*An undulating belt of green coastal bush and forest, slashed by cool mountain streams and bordered by jagged seaside cliffs, extends along the length of the Tsitsikamma Coastal National Park, between Nature's Valley in the west and the mouth of the Groot River. Hiking trails traversing this rugged coastline explore a wonderland of indigenous ferns, trees and flowers, and provide panoramic mountain-top views of dolphins and whales basking in the shimmering waters of the Indian Ocean. Underwater trails reveal the brilliant colours and diversity of the Tsitsikamma's submarine fauna and flora proliferating in the open sea and rocky, tidal pools that fringe the shore.*

*A breaking wave performs a sun-dance on the southern coast.*

*A rocky peninsula piercing the warm waters of the Indian Ocean protects the waters of Stilbaai, a popular southern Cape fishing resort.*

*The Nuweveld Mountains command sweeping views of the Karoo National Park, where erosion has carved furrows in the landscape.*

*Giant walls of rock tower above a green valley near Prince Albert.*

## FOLLOWING THE ZEBRA TRAIL

*In the high Karoo country of the Mountain Zebra National Park, hiking trails cross an elevated landscape that rises to 1957 metres at Spitskop, the highest point in the park. Here, on the grassy northern slopes of the Bankberg, and on the adjacent plateaux, roams a variety of game, including eland, springbok, black wildebeest, red hartebeest, and about 200 of one of the world's rarest mammals, the mountain zebra. Hiking trails traverse beautiful gorges formed by mountain streams, and provide panoramic views of distant mountain peaks and sweeping valleys.*

*Partly camouflaged by morning mist, mountains loom above the grassy countryside in the Mountain Zebra National Park.*

*Resembling the fossilised bones of primeval creatures, these mountain folds near Oudtshoorn reveal a symmetry ancient and beautiful.*

*Pale-blue skies, crisp air and vast plains interrupted by flat-topped mountains combine to make the Karoo a land of enduring tranquillity.*

*An ocean of mist eddies and swirls around the flanks of flat-topped hills in the Karoo.*

*The gentle yellow and brown shades of the Karoo are reflected in this arid landscape of kraalbos (Galenia africana) and odd-shaped hills.*

*Ancient boulders of the Karoo soak up the sun in their dry, dusty environment. Karoo is an old Khoikhoi word which means 'land of thirst'.*

*Like sun-bronzed sentinels, these imposing pillars of rock soar above the parched plains of the Valley of Desolation in the Great Karoo.*

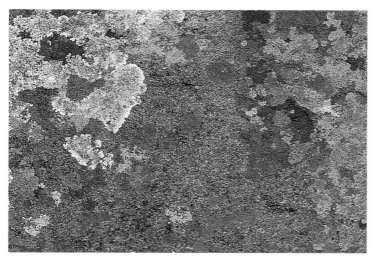

*A masterpiece in lichen and rock in the Karoo Nature Reserve.*

## GRAND VIEWS OVER A DESOLATE VALLEY

*Majestic pillars of weathered dolerite cap the shale heights above the Valley of Desolation near Graaff-Reinet. These dolerite formations, eroded into a multitude of bizarre and grotesque shapes, rise to heights of 120 metres above the seemingly endless plains of the Karoo as it stretches out to the northern foothills of the Grootrivier and Klein-Winterhoek mountains. The heights above the Valley of Desolation also overlook the Sundays River as it curls around Graaff-Reinet, and the fortress of rock known as Spandau Kop.*

*Fired by the golden rays of the rising sun, jagged turrets of rock loom above the stark wilderness of the Karoo's Valley of Desolation.*

*A giant crack which snakes through the Swartberg range has formed a passageway between the Little Karoo and its northern hinterland.*

## MOUNTAINS CLEFT BY PASSES

*The Swartberg range is the cradle for three of the world's most enchanting mountain passes. Here tributaries of the Gouritz River have slashed fissures up to 1 000 metres deep through the hard sandstone, creating a spectacle of dark kloofs flanked by precipitous cliffs and giant, soaring peaks.*
*The Meiringspoort Pass, following the course of the Groot River, crosses it 26 times through the mountains, while the Swartberg Pass climbs 1 400 metres over slopes covered with proteas, ericas and watsonias. Another majestic crack through the Swartberg is the Seweweekspoort. Washed by the waters of mountain streams, and inhabited by a variety of small animals, reptiles and insects, this is one of southern Africa's most beautiful mountain drives.*

*Immense pressures beneath the earth's crust created these dramatic folds in the Swartberge.*

*Erosion over millennia has worked away at the upfolded masses of the Swartberg range, creating wrinkles and scars along its face.*

*Kokerboom bark: a landscape of peaks and shadowy valleys.*

*A quiver tree (kokerboom) towers above the ground.*

From the towering yellowwoods of the Tsitsikamma forests in
the south to the gnarled baobabs of the northern Transvaal, the
trees and forests of South Africa serve not only as a haven for
birds, animals and insects, but also as a continual source of
inspiration and peace for the embattled spirit of man.

The subjects of this priceless kingdom of trees include about
1 000 indigenous species, covering the land in a variety of
incredible contrasts. From the twisted branches of the wild
green-hair tree to the silky leaves of the graceful silver tree is an
endless spectrum of changing colours and forms. Saffrons and
cycads; acacias and willows; milkwoods, mulberries and elms;
fever and fig trees; ebony and beech — all have a special place
on the subcontinent of southern Africa.

*Sycamore fig trees bask in early sunlight in the Kruger Park.*

*Tentacle-like roots of an African rock fig tree claw the ground.*

*A waterlogged, ancient fig tree bends under the weight of years.*

*Monarch of the Tsitsikamma forest: the Outeniqua yellowwood.*

*These dying leaves will generate new life in the Tsitsikamma.*

*Candelabra-shaped kaoko euphorbia trees stand stiffly erect on the rocky slopes of the Baynes Mountains in northern Namibia.*

*Age-old giants of the Knysna forest, some a thousand years old, create a luxurious canopy of green stretching further than the eye can see.*

# IN THE THIRSTLANDS OF THE NORTH

*T*HE NORTHERN CAPE *is the Cinderella of southern Africa: dry, dusty and drought-stricken over much of its arid plains for most of the year, its coastline becomes a floral wonderland, ablaze with magnificent colours in spring. To the north, the sun-baked thirstlands of the Richtersveld and Bushmanland taper off into abundant green valleys on the banks of the Orange — the 'Great River' of the San and Khoikhoi. Here the roar of the river tumbling into its granite gorge at the Augrabies Falls reverberates above the stillness of the surrounding alluvial terraces. Further north, in the Kalahari Desert, ochre sand dunes, fringed with acacia and kameeldoring, merge with dry watercourses that disappear in the shimmering heat.*

*Moving southwards to the Great Karoo, the landscape changes. Here endless plains, peppered with stunted hills and strange-shaped rocks, stretch from one horizon to another, embracing sunrises in red, orange and gold. Buried beneath this drought-stricken landscape are the fossil remains of mammal-like reptiles that stalked the land more than 200 million years ago. Further west, the rugged peaks of the Cedarberg tower 1 800 metres above a land cleft by rivers and streams. In this tranquil region, sandstone arches, hollowed out by wind and rain, form grotesque sculptures on mountain tops, and proteas flourish above the snow line, inviting nature lovers to their colourful, cool environment.*

*Jagged rocks of the Great Karoo reflect the copper rays of the sun, in a landscape that covers fossils more than 200 million years old.*

*A wild iris in granite near Kamieskroon.*

## THE KAROO'S TIMELESS LANDSCAPE

*Karoo is the Khoikhoi word for 'land of thirst', a drought-stricken region of vast, sparsely-vegetated plains reaching out to distant horizons. Here, on the southern part of South Africa's great central plateau, isolated homesteads, flat-topped hills and jagged rocks are the only landmarks in the immensity of open spaces. Along the steep, shale sides of these flat-topped hills are the fossil remains of mammal-like reptiles such as* Tapinocephalus, Cistecephalus *and* Lystrosaurus, *that lived on the plains between 240 and 190 million years ago, when enormous outpourings of volcanic lava buried them alive.*

*Long shadows cover the sparse scrubland of the Karoo.*

*Cursed by drought, the parched, semidesert plains of the northern Cape near Pofadder stretch out to distant mountains.*

*Shadows creep across the undulating mountain slopes of northern Namaqualand, like dark islands in a land flooded by sunshine.*

*A Namaqualand quiver tree (kokerboom), its branches like gnarled fingers pointing at the sun, stands alone on its rocky terrace.*

*A cluster of isolated hills rises up from the golden plains near Aggeneys, a sandy wilderness where drought has become a way of life.*

## NAMAQUALAND'S SPRINGTIME WONDERLAND

*The arid, wind-blown wastes of Namaqualand, pampered by the meagre rains of late winter, explode in a frenzy of growth, as millions of wild flowers carpet the land in one of the earth's great botanical extravaganzas. As if grateful for the cooling relief after months of drought, these flowers spring from the ground with remarkable haste, creating rolling seas of vibrant colour. The reds and yellows of Namaqualand daisies merge with the brilliant mauves and purples of everlastings and cinerarias, while innumerable other species rustle in the whispering winds of spring.*

*The wild flower* Dipidax triquetra *in the Biedouw Valley.*

*Wild flowers form an enchanting carpet of colour near the Biedouw Valley, as the Cedarberg range looms in the background.*

*Rejuvenated by rain and the promise of spring, the arid plains of Namaqualand become floral oceans, ablaze with a variety of colours.*

*The sculpted rock formations of the Cedarberg tumble down into a wilderness of unspoilt valleys washed by crystal-clear streams.*

*The Cedarberg is a wonderland of bizarre sandstone shapes, wrinkled, dented or rounded by the weathering of its weak parts.*

*Bronzed by the sun, fashioned by the wind and rain, the Cedarberg's Wolfberg Arch is a spectacular example of the great powers of erosion.*

*In an amphitheatre of towering mountains, the Wolfberg Arch has its own unique majesty.*

## MAGIC OF THE CEDARBERG

*Spectacular rock formations, eroded by wind and rain over millions of years, rise up out of the craggy mountains of the Cedarberg. Pinnacles, pillars, arches, halls, caves and lofty crosses have been carved out of the quartz-sandstone of the region — an unspoilt wilderness bisected by deep valleys, and dominated by tall peaks. Outstanding formations are the Wolfberg Arch, the Maltese Cross and the Stadsaal, or 'town hall' — a mass of rock honeycombed with corridors, caves, chambers and crevices.*

*The Wolfberg Arch crowns the Wolfberg Mountains at 1 608 metres, forming a natural eye in the crisp, blue skies of the Cedarberg.*

*With a mighty roar, the hurtling waters of the Orange River plunge precipitously into a gorge at the Augrabies Falls in the northern Cape.*

## NOISY INFERNO OF WATER

*Known to the Khoikhoi as Aukoerebis ('the place of great noise'), the mighty Augrabies Falls are regarded as one of the six greatest waterfalls in the world. Here, between precipitous walls of granite, 3 000 million years old, the Orange River reveals the full fury of its raging waters as they burst over the edge of the falls into the seething gorge below. In times of flood, the waters of the Orange above the falls are braided into smaller channels of water which tumble into the gorge as multiple waterfalls, creating a remarkable spectacle of thundering water.*

*The sound of thunder rumbles through spray in the rocky flanks of the Augrabies Falls.*

*Uniting at the head of the Augrabies Falls, the main streams of the Orange burst over the edge and plummet 146 metres to the pool below.*

## SUMPTUOUS GARDEN IN THE DESERT

*The waters of the Orange bring life and colour to the parched plains of the northern Cape. Along the river's banks in the Augrabies Falls National Park, the rolling semidesert is transformed into a fertile garden teeming with life. Here the sandy wastes become belts of rich green, supporting a variety of plants and trees, including willow, kokerboom, acacia, wild olive and haworthia.*

*The river tumbles through its gorge for 10 kilometres, descending some 350 metres in a series of rapids. On the way, several tributary gorges unite with the turbulent river, vastly increasing the volume of its churning, swirling waters as they head towards the sea.*

*Cliffs tower 120 metres above the turbulence at Augrabies Falls.*

*The Orange River has slashed a spectacular gorge through walls of black and grey granite in the Augrabies Falls National Park.*

*The prehistoric shapes of the Riemvasmaak Mountains dominate a rocky wilderness in the Augrabies Falls National Park.*

*Bewitching contours ripple across the Kalahari's dune sea.*

*The sprawling wilderness of the Kalahari Gemsbok National Park is home to 10 000 springbok, as well as a variety of other game.*

*Cirrus clouds streak across a brooding sky, high above the rugged Kalahari landscape of grassland, sand dunes and thorn trees.*

*The Orange River near Sendelingsdrift.*

*Hundreds of bush-covered, sandy islands split the swirling waters of the Orange River on its twisting journey below Upington.*

*Dune vegetation fringes the coastline near Lambert's Bay on the west coast, breeding ground of penguins, cormorants and gannets.*

*Every year, the sterile, drought-stricken countryside of Namaqualand, fed by rain and the promise of spring, is transformed into a floral wonderland, creating a rich, multicoloured garden on the very doorstep of the Namib Desert. In a stunning surge of growth between mid-July and September, species after species spring from the ground in their millions, making Namaqualand a mecca for nature lovers all over South Africa.*

*A posy of rare beauty,* Colpias mollis.

*The magic flowers of Namaqualand transform this parched land into a springtime paradise, setting the countryside ablaze with colour.*

*A canopy of vibrant colours fringes the secluded shores of the Langebaan lagoon.*

*Namaqualand's daisies face the sun.*

*A shimmering sheet of white, green and gold covers the ground in the Nieuwoudtville Nature Reserve in Namaqualand.*

*The leaves of* Leucadendron daphnoides *in tantalising shades of white, green and red.*

*Clustered white flower heads of* Brunia albiflora *at Hermanus.*

*The royal countenance of the king protea* (P. cynaroides).

*Cosmos blooms transform dull fields into carpets of riotous colour in autumn.*

*Hundreds of dainty, forked white flowers of the Cape pond weed (waterblommetjie) bring a springtime fragrance to the southwestern Cape.*

# TRANQUIL LAND OF THE SETTLERS

*H*ERE IS THE QUIET CORNER *of southern Africa, a frontierland of exquisite beauty, forged by the pioneering spirit of man. From the Storms River in the south to the Mtamvuna River on Natal's border in the north, the variety of this region's startling landscapes is perhaps greater than anywhere else on the subcontinent.*

*In the south, the rich green slopes of the Suurberge tumble down through valleys carpeted with citrus trees, to the bush and grasslands of settler country. Here, nature reserves harbouring elephant, white rhino, buffalo and wildebeest retain the spirit of the past when great herds roamed the region before the advent of man.*

*Further east, church spires rise up in towns hidden between the folds of undulating hills, beacons of an age enshrined by old forts, historic homesteads and wagon tracks. Here in aloe country, far south of the snow-capped peaks and trout streams of the Amatole Mountains, lazy rivers creep through canyons and pineapple-covered hills towards the sea. And all along the coastline, tiny hamlets bask beside the banks of these waterways, watching the ebb and flow of the tides, and the rich variety of birds that flock to feed upon the food they bring.*

*In Transkei, rustic settlements perched on hills of velvet green look out across ribbons of wild, white sand fringed by rich, subtropical vegetation. This region is a true nature lovers' paradise, where creeper-draped forests hug the coast, camouflaging a vibrant world of birds, insects and tiny animals; where waterfalls plunge into the deep-blue sea; and huge fortresses of rock rise up from the surf — rugged monuments to the destructive force of time itself.*

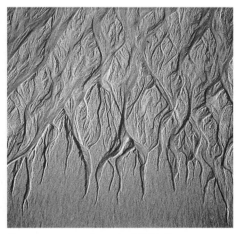

*Patterns in sand on the Wild Coast.*

*Framed by undulating hills, the tranquil waters of the Indian Ocean wash an unspoilt coastline near Port St Johns on the Wild Coast.*

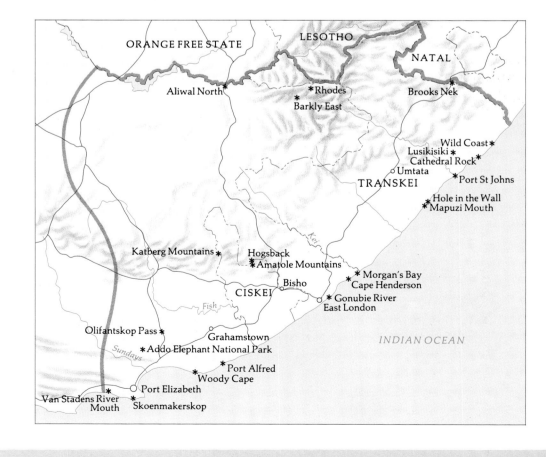

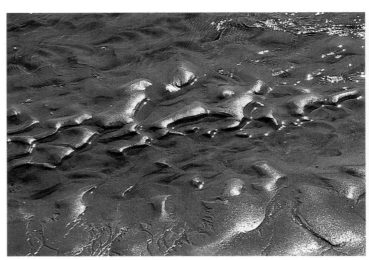

*The sun adds a dazzling sheen to the sands of the Wild Coast.*

*Leaden skies hang low over the Indian Ocean's moody coastline near the Van Stadens River mouth. This area is a popular fishing haunt.*

*Sun-bleached sand dunes, crowned with turrets of coastal bush, flank the Van Stadens River, which forms a shallow lagoon at its mouth.*

*A wilderness of huge dunes and long stretches of white sand taper off to meet the Indian Ocean east of the town of Port Alfred.*

*Shimmering sands fringe the mouth of the Great Kei north of Morgan's Bay. The river is the boundary between Transkei and Ciskei.*

*The movement of the tides has created a landscape of wrinkles and corrugations in the copper sands lining the mouth of the Kei River.*

## ON THE STRANDLOPER TRAIL

*The eastern Cape coastline is well known for its wide, lazy rivers which snake through a landscape of bush-covered mountains and tumble out of sleepy estuaries into the sparkling sea. Attracted to the cool, luxuriant bush and forests flanking these rivers is a startling variety of birds. Here, on the fringe of the Indian Ocean, gulls, cormorants, oystercatchers and terns rub shoulders with fish eagles and storks, spoonbills and sand plovers. On land, bushbuck and blue duiker inhabit the thickets, while beneath the waves that wash these shores cruise silent denizens of the deep: great white and hammerhead sharks chasing tasty morsels of multicoloured fish.*

*Covered by a luxuriant canopy of green, this fortress of rock looms above the swirling waters of the Gonubie River north of East London.*

One of the beach's bizarre landscapes.

Translucent waters teeming with sea-life wash the coastline near Skoenmakerskop. Ancient shipwrecks lie beneath these waters.

## WILD MOODS OF THE TRANSKEI COAST

*Transkei's Wild Coast, stretching from the Kei River in the south to the Mtamvuna River in the north, is a wonderland of emerald hills rolling down to a turquoise sea; of white ribbons of sand embraced by fringes of subtropical green. Here, rocky headlands thrust majestically into the sea, creating tranquil bays and windless beaches. But when the weather turns bad, the mood of the Wild Coast changes, and the sea, whipped up into a raging cauldron of white water, batters the coast with a booming crescendo of sound, making it a dangerous and inhospitable place for animals and man.*

*A dome of grass-covered rock, framed by rich coastal vegetation, rears above the vast expanse of the Indian Ocean at Mapuzi Mouth.*

*Illuminated by the sun, the rolling hills of the Wild Coast bare their graceful curves to the roaring waters of a restless sea.*

*Waves create a seething mantle of white near Morgan's Bay.*

*The gentle curves of the eastern Cape coast near Woody Cape embrace a graceful hinterland of sun-drenched dunes and dense, coastal bush.*

*Backdropped by the rugged eastern Cape interior, ivory sands form a barrier between the Indian Ocean and a lagoon at Cape Henderson.*

## HOLE IN THE WALL

*The mighty roar of the sea rushing through a tunnel in an island of rock off the Wild Coast inspired the earliest inhabitants of Transkei to call it esiKhaleni — 'the place of sound'. To later arrivals, witnessing the spectacle of white water thundering through this sandstone fortress, this strange geologic phenomenon became known as 'Hole in the Wall'. And so it remains to this day, remarkable evidence of the staggering power of water to gouge a path through rock.*

*The sea has bored a tunnel through this sandstone island at Hole in the Wall, creating one of the great natural wonders of southern Africa.*

*Rocky spires reach skyward above Cathedral Rock, a magnificent sandstone monument, sculpted by the waves over millions of years.*

*Fringed by willow and poplar trees, a river weaves a graceful path through mountains and pastures near Brooks Nek.*

*Undulating hills, swathed in grasslands of gold, reach down to a sparkling farm dam near the town of Barkly East in the northeastern Cape.*

*Stately hills peer down on the swirling waters of the Igoda River as it meanders through an attractive valley on its way to the sea.*

*Emerald folds of the Katberg Mountains disappear into deep, forested valleys, once the scene of bitter fighting during the frontier wars.*

*Ghostly trunks in a Hogsback forest.*

## MOUNTAINS IN THE MIST

*A remote region of mountain peaks, misty forests and cascading streams falling down to fertile valleys lies at the western end of the Amatole Mountains in the eastern Cape. This area, known as Hogsback, is believed to have been named after one of the area's mountain ridges, whose spiky summit resembles the bristles of a hog's back. Here, rustic trails, fringed with ferns and flowers, lead through forests of yellowwood, white ironwood, assegai and cabbage trees to rocky promontories looking up to the towering peaks of the Amatole range.*

*Rustling grasslands and clusters of bush provide a landscape of rustic charm near Rhodes, in the shadow of the southern Drakensberg.*

*Sun-splashed giants in a sea of green, these two African elephants lumber through bush in the Addo Elephant National Park.*

*Stretching northwards from the Olifantskop Pass, the bushland of the eastern Cape presents a landscape of rolling hills and valleys.*

*Luxuriant forest and barren grassland contrast sharply beneath the majestic countenance of a towering mountain giant near Kokstad.*

*The Amatole Mountains loom high above pine forests.*

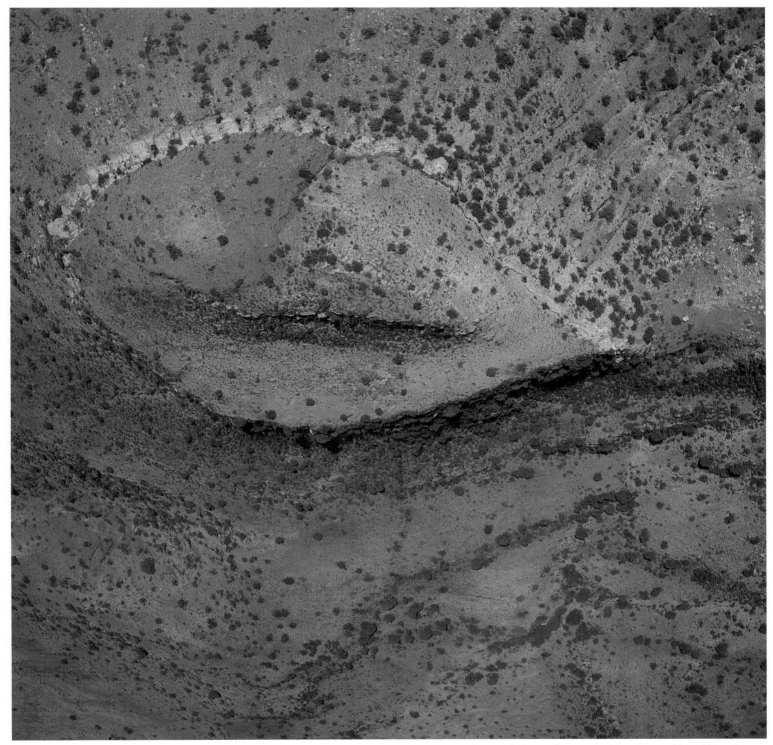

*Like a barren eye dried out by the relentless rays of the sun, a desolate hill looms skywards from the parched land near Aliwal North.*

*Sparkling rivers cascading over waterfalls slash the beautiful mountains of Transkei on their panoramic journey to the Indian Ocean.*

*After traversing the grassy downland country near Lusikisiki, the cool waters of the Magwa River plunge 142 metres into a narrow gorge.*

*To a symphony of changing colours, seabirds perform a twilight dance above kelp beds near Kommetjie on the Atlantic coast.*

The world of southern Africa's birds, from the tiny penduline tit to the flightless ostrich, encompasses a breathtaking variety of species. More than one tenth of the world's avian population live here in a land of bizarre climatic and topographic differences. They have adapted to habitats from the Namib Desert to the dunes of the southern Cape coast, from the dusty plains of the Doring Karoo to the peaks of the Lebombo Mountains. Included in the panoply of winged beauty is a vast family of weaverbirds, waxbills and widowbirds; tiny thrushes and chats; eagles and hawks; and a colourful world of loeries, lovebirds and parrots.

Adding to the vast treasure chest of indigenous birds is an ever-changing cosmopolitan population of intercontinental migrants, bringing new life and colour to the shores of the subcontinent in summer.

Jackass penguins face the Atlantic's icy surge on Malgas Island.

Common terns give a ragged aerial display above the waters of Hermanus lagoon. They usually hover before diving for small fish.

*Gannets groom each other on Bird Island, Lambert's Bay. Elegant curves and striking plumage compensate for their raucous behaviour.*

*Showing grace and elegance in flight, a gannet leaves its colony and heads for the sea.*

*A giant eagle owl stares down from its woodland perch.*

*Striking architect of the wild... a lesser masked weaver.*

*The wattled plover, feathered sovereign in a kingdom of grass.*

# LAND IN THE LAP OF THE DRAGON

*F*ROM THE MIGHTY HORNS *of the Drakensberg to the smooth, undulating hills and emerald valleys that reach down to her subtropical shores, Natal is a province of enchanting, rustic beauty. Traditionally known as the 'garden province', this region is the ultimate dreamer's refuge — a tranquil mix of mountain landscapes, quiet country fields, game reserves and dazzling ribbons of white sand fringing luxuriant coastal bush and forests.*

*In the south, interspersed with groves of lala palms and wild banana trees, forests of Natal mahogany, wild fig and marula trees create a home for monkeys and a fragrant setting for ferns, orchids and multicoloured lilies. Along the north coast, the turquoise waters and lazy sands of holiday resorts merge with the coastal fringe, giving way to sugar cane fields and the rolling hills of Zululand.*

*To the west, the mighty Mgeni River meanders through the Valley of a Thousand Hills, a breathtaking landscape of tumbling slopes and deep, narrow valleys. Further inland, the scented grasslands of the midlands reach down to the verges of tranquil country lakes and dams, and icy rivers born in the Drakensberg.*

*The Drakensberg itself, created millions of years ago, broods above the rest of southern Africa, an enigmatic and monumental signpost pointing the way to the garden province.*

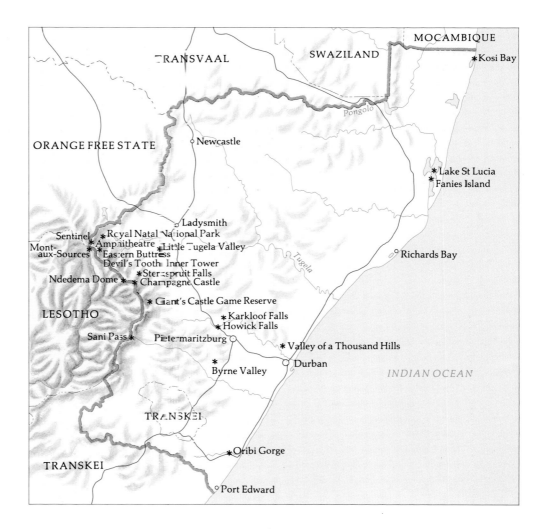

*The Drakensberg's Ndedema Dome towers gracefully above emerald valleys which tumble down into Natal from the highlands of Lesotho.*

*Ridges plunge down to mysterious valleys near the Sani Pass.*

*The eroded flanks of the Drakensberg reach out to the valley floor, in a landscape dominated by sunlight and shadows.*

*Drakensberg peaks pierce the sky high above the Mkhomazana River valley. The Sani Pass follows the Mkhomazana's upper valley.*

*A break in the mist reveals the rugged grandeur of precipitous mountains plunging to green valleys near the Oribi Gorge in southern Natal.*

*The Mzimkulwana River snakes its way through a wilderness of creepers, trees and plants at Horseshoe Bend near the Oribi Gorge.*

*Pierced by the dazzling rays of the sun, a secluded waterfall in the Natal Drakensberg becomes a radiant torrent of sparkling water.*

*Thundering waters of the Howick Falls.*

## THE MIGHTY MGENI'S ROAR OF THUNDER

*Rising on the slopes of the 2146-metre Spioenkop, the Mgeni River splashes through the gentle grasslands of the Natal midlands until, near Howick, in a torrent of roaring white water, it plunges 102 metres headlong into a gorge. These magnificent falls, with their precipitous, bush-fringed flanks, were known to the earliest inhabitants of the area as kwaNogqaza ('place of the tall one'). The Mgeni's waters just above the Howick Falls mark the fording point of settlers and travellers in oxwagons, some of whom were swept to their deaths over the edge of the falls.*

*A narrow sheet of white water tumbles over a precipitous ledge and hurtles 115 metres into a gorge at the Karkloof Falls near Howick.*

*A majestic wall of basalt rock, reaching more than 3000 metres in height, looms above the valleys of the Giant's Castle Game Reserve.*

*Icy waters lunge towards a yawning chasm at the Sterkspruit Falls.*

## GIANT PEAKS BATTERED BY STORMS

*The great basalt wall of the Drakensberg stretches southwards from Cathkin Peak at a height of more than 3 000 metres — a dark, jagged barrier slashed by the courses of countless rivers and streams. At Giant's Castle, this wall climbs even higher to 3 314 metres to form a monumental cornerstone overlooking the Giant's Castle Game Reserve. Known to the Zulus as iNtabayikonjwa ('the mountain at which one must not point'), Giant's Castle witnesses the full fury of summer's electrical storms, echoing the roll of thunder through the Drakensberg and reflecting the jagged lightning which soars across its peaks.*

*Backdropped by mighty mountains, an undulating carpet of golden-green grass covers the terraces in the Giant's Castle Game Reserve.*

*Chill blue waters of a country dam reflect the great basalt heights of the Drakensberg. Champagne Castle, at 3 348 metres, is in the centre.*

*A canopy of lush, green grass and wild flowers in the Little Tugela Valley creates a picturesque setting in the Drakensberg.*

*Jagged, snow-clad peaks pierce the sky in the Drakensberg. In summer these peaks reverberate with the roar of thunderstorms.*

*Caught in a blaze of sunlight, Clarens sandstone ridges bring shimmering shades of gold, orange and red to the foothills of the Drakensberg.*

*The mighty Sentinel, marking the northern end of the main Drakensberg at 3165 metres, rears above the summit of the Amphitheatre.*

*A lonely road bisects rolling grasslands near the Royal Natal National Park. The park is renowned for its magnificent scenery.*

## NATURE'S AWESOME AMPHITHEATRE

*A rugged wall of rock four kilometres wide towers above the
Royal Natal National Park in the northwestern corner of the
province. Known as the Amphitheatre, this massive basalt cliff
face is flanked by two mighty pillars of rock: the Eastern
Buttress on the left, and the Sentinel on the right. These
mountain giants are remnants of a great volcanic crust that
once extended to the coast, and which has been eroded by
rivers over millions of years — since Africa broke away from
the supercontinent Gondwanaland. Today the majesty of these
mountains in the Drakensberg attracts visitors worldwide, their
lofty heights exposing panoramic vistas stretching to distant
horizons.*

*The brooding grandeur of the Sentinel's basalt rock face radiates across a land of mountain giants in the Royal Natal National Park.*

*The majestic Amphitheatre of the Mont-aux-Sources reaches skywards. The Sentinel is on the right, the Eastern Buttress on the left.*

## ICY RIVERS IN A MOUNTAIN PARADISE

*Cool yellowwood forests, waterfalls, shady gorges and picturesque paths traversing basalt ridges lure nature lovers and hikers to the Royal Natal National Park. Once the domain of San hunters, the hills and valleys below the huge peaks are home to a variety of animals and birds. These creatures draw sustenance from the icy waters of rivers and streams which have their sources high up in the Drakensberg. The most awesome of these is the Tugela River which drops 3000 metres in a series of spectacular falls and cascades to the valley floor. One of these falls, 614 metres tall, is the highest in South Africa, while the combined drop of the Tugela Falls makes it the second highest waterfall in the world.*

*The Eastern Buttress, Devil's Tooth and the Inner Tower rise proudly above the clouds, monuments to ancient geologic upheavals.*

*Rolling hills, forested glens and the crisp, clean air of the Natal midlands provide a tranquil environment for weary visitors.*

*Bush-covered mountains tumble down to fertile valleys created by tributaries of the Mgeni River in the Valley of a Thousand Hills.*

*Gentle, forested hills flank the rustic Byrne Valley near Richmond — named after British immigrants who settled in the area in 1850.*

Pink blossoms herald spring in the foothills of the Drakensberg. Summer will cast a green mantle over this land browned by the cold.

Against a backdrop of distant mountains, colourful meadows and maize fields form a patchwork of serene beauty in the Natal midlands.

*Rustling fields of sugar cane resemble rolling carpets of green across the picturesque hills and valleys fringing the Natal coastline.*

*Twisting curves crisscross sugar cane fields near the Tugela River.*

*Billowing puffs of cumulus cloud float like airships across the sultry fields of sugar cane that dominate the coastlands of Natal.*

## SUBTROPICAL SEAS OF GREEN

*A vast, undulating sea of sugar cane stretches northwards along the coastal belt from Durban to the Tugela River. Extending some 50 km inland, this belt of green was once a luxuriant coastal forest teeming with small animals, a multitude of snakes and countless tropical plants and flowers. Today, while much of this coastal forest has disappeared, the soft sands of the north coast are fringed with palms and exotic flowering plants, and vervet monkeys still find shelter in the deep recesses of the tangled bush.*

*The idyllic coastline near Port Edward.*

*A gentle sweep of luxuriant coastal forest and sand separates the warm waters of the Indian Ocean and the broad lakes of Kosi Bay.*

*Framed by rolling fields of sugar cane, the sands of the Natal coastline slip beneath the shimmering waters of the Indian Ocean.*

*The radiant light of a new day filtering through a sea mist dazzles the tawny sands of an isolated beach on the Natal south coast.*

*A silver sea washes the sands of Natal's north coast. Once a passageway for shipwrecked sailors, the coast now is a tourists' paradise.*

## A SHALLOW LAKE TEEMING WITH LIFE

*Lake St Lucia on the Natal north coast is a tranquil retreat for nature lovers, bird-watchers, hikers and anglers. The mud flats, reeds and coastal bush around the lake are home to an astonishing variety of bird life — including the magnificent pink-backed pelican which breeds there. About 2 000 crocodiles and 700 hippo wallow in the lake's shallow waters, and large numbers of freshwater, estuarine and marine fish breed here too. Four parks surrounding the lake are a haven for monkeys, reedbuck, buffalo, waterbuck, impala, nyala and kudu.*

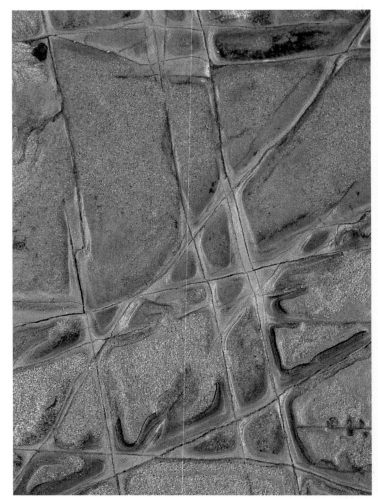

*Erosion has etched unique, linear patterns on the face of this rock.*

*Rain clouds pile up high above the delicate curves of Natal's north coast near Lake St Lucia, home of hippo, crocodile and aquatic birds.*

*The placid waters of Lake St Lucia lap the grassy shores of Fanies Island. The area is a natural sanctuary for about 360 bird species.*

*A winter blanket of snow and mist covers these ancient mountains in the Karoo's Mountain Zebra National Park.*

*Crusty patches of lichen form an island in a sea of snow.*

*Thunderstorms bring welcome relief to sun-baked summer days in the Kruger National Park. Here an impala has an impromptu shower.*

*Hungry flames devour the trunk and branches of an acacia tree stranded in the veld.*

*Lashed by gale-force winds, young eucalyptus trees bend towards the blazing heat of an uncontrollable fire, as sparks fly in all directions.*

*A forest fire wreaks havoc in a eucalyptus plantation. These trees stand impassive in their final seconds as a wall of flame advances.*

# ROLLING PLAINS SPLASHED BY THE SUN

*F ROM THE GRASSLANDS and maize fields that merge with the willow-lined banks of the Vaal River in the south, to the rocky ridges of the Magaliesberg and the granite outcrops of the Pilanesberg in the north, the southern Transvaal is a region of wide open spaces, crisp, clean air and deep blue skies.*

*Once the domain of mighty herds of game, this region is one of the world's great treasure chests of underground wealth — a priceless vault of minerals, metals and precious stones, deposited millions of years ago through cataclysmic geologic forces. Here the great adventures of the gold rush were played out as fortune hunters dug deep, seeking wealth and instant fame.*

*Today, in spite of the intrusions of man, the southern Transvaal has retained the rustic mood that was so typical of the Highveld centuries ago. In the north, beneath the granite outcrops of the Pilanesberg, wooded areas, natural lakes and forested ravines provide a tranquil setting for rhino, kudu, duiker, giraffe, leopard and other animals. East of the Pilanesberg, the ancient Magaliesberg range looms above the shimmering waters of Hartbeespoort Dam, its cliffs a canvas of prehistoric art, and its ledges a home for Cape vultures, monkeys and baboons. To the west, the slumbering citrus valleys of the Groot-Marico River recall the pioneering days of the Voortrekkers and the characters that succeeded them, immortalised in the works of Herman Charles Bosman.*

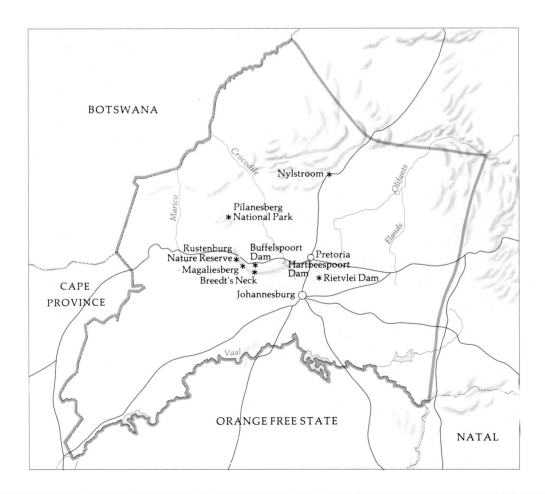

*Fleecy cumulus clouds cast dark shadows over maize fields and golden grasslands in the southern Transvaal.*

*Pregnant with rain, thunderclouds gather ominously above thick grassland and bush country near Nylstroom in the southern Transvaal.*

*A carpet of golden grass fringes the tranquil banks of the Rietvlei Dam in the Riebeeck Nature Reserve near Verwoerdburg.*

*A skirt of dense bush hugs the granite flanks of this koppie, one of several in the popular Pilanesberg National Park, Bophuthatswana.*

## AN ANCIENT VOLCANIC COUNTRY

*The Pilanesberg area was born in a spectacular volcanic eruption, which broke through the rock of the Bushveld Complex about 1 290 million years ago. Today, the hills of the Pilanesberg are the crumbling foundations of the crater through which this eruption took place. The centre of the crater, which rises some 600 metres above the surrounding countryside, today forms a beautiful setting for a man-made lake called 'Mankwe' — the place of the leopard. This lake is a watering hole for numerous species of game, ranging from white rhino and hippo to elephant and buffalo.*

*A waterhole in the Pilanesberg National Park reflects the rustic beauty of the bushveld, a haven for a variety of animals and birds.*

## EXCAVATIONS ON THE ROCK FACE

*Mighty torrents of water have scooped out formidable ravines and chasms from the rocky face of the Magaliesberg over the years. Today, these wooded ravines and the streams which plunge over the quartzite cliffs are a major attraction in the Rustenburg Nature Reserve, which lies on the plateau and northern flanks of the Magaliesberg.*

*Here, crystal-clear rock pools provide watering holes for mountain reedbuck and sable, springbok and eland, red hartebeest, blesbok and kudu, while the unspoilt wilderness of trees and bush also serves as home to a colourful family of more than 140 bird species.*

*An unspoilt wilderness of wooded ravines and rocky kloofs sprawls across the Magaliesberg in the Rustenburg Nature Reserve.*

*Grimacing quartzite boulders in the Rustenburg Nature Reserve.*

*The rocky, grass-covered hills of the Magaliesberg roll northwards, from Breedt's Nek to Buffelspoort Dam in the distance.*

*A sparkling river dances through an enchanting wooded ravine in the Magaliesberg, home of monkeys, baboons, duiker and steenbok.*

*Jagged cliffs of sunburnt rock tumble down to evergreen gorges in the Magaliesberg. The region has a wealth of rock engravings.*

*The gentle peaks of the Magaliesberg range loom eerily through a shroud of mist.*

*The sloping foothills of the Magaliesberg unfold to reveal the shimmering waters of Hartbeespoort Dam, west of Pretoria.*

## THE MOUNTAINS OF MAGALI

*The quartzite scarps of the Magaliesberg, running in an almost
unbroken line along the crests of gentle hills from the east of
Pretoria to the west of Rustenburg, have witnessed the
decimation of mighty herds of elephant and antelope in the last
150 years. Today, however, in spite of the predations of man
over the years, animals such as duiker, steenbok, oribi,
monkey, baboon and brown hyena still inhabit the wooded
ravines and the gentle, bushy slopes.*

*The name Magaliesberg means 'Magali's Mountain'. Magali
was a chief of the Po people who lived in the area at the time the
Voortrekkers arrived during the 19th century.*

*Under a canopy of clouds, rocky grasslands in the Magaliesberg sweep down to valleys scoured out by erosion over the years.*

## WONDERS OF THE LIVING SKY

*The atmosphere and open spaces above our planet form a marvellous amphitheatre in which nature performs some of her finest works of art. In southern Africa, particularly, the skies reflect the endless march of time and the miracle of living things: heaved banks of cumulonimbus raincloud exploding in a Karoo sky; blood-red sunsets over the ochre sands of the Kalahari; a pale moon rising above the Indian Ocean; the light of distant galaxies illuminating the skies of the southern coast — such are the wonders brought to us through the living sky.*

*Billowing cumulus clouds form a natural staircase to the heavens near Witbank in the Transvaal.*

*Like a brilliant splash of gold in a deep-blue sky, cumulonimbus clouds merge with high cirrus clouds during a Highveld thunderstorm.*

*Suffused with the startling colours of dawn, patches of stratocumulus cloud flee before the rising sun on the Natal South Coast.*

*Gigantic columns of cumulus cloud form a fleecy shield against the sun.*

*Appearing like frosted glass, these altostratus clouds stretch across the afternoon sky, producing a panorama of changing colours.*

*Low-lying stratus cloud blankets the slopes of the Drakensberg Mountains in Natal. These layered clouds often bring drizzle.*

# LAND WHERE THE BAOBAB IS KING

*T*HE NORTHERN TRANSVAAL, *country of the baobab, home of some of the oldest rocks on earth, living museum of momentous geologic forces, is a region of staggering contrasts. Flattened by a creeping lake of molten rock that undermined its ragged surface about 600 million years ago, the southern part is a vast plain of rich red soil, savannah and thorn trees, stretching northwards to the distant horns of the Strydpoortberg and Waterberg ranges.*

*Further north, the grassy Pietersburg plateau descends eastwards to a region of mystical beauty and enduring charm. Here giant ironwood and redwood trees, kiepersol and cabbage trees reach up to the sun on the emerald slopes of the Woodbush Mountains, and samango monkeys and lynxes, bushbuck and wild pigs seek shelter within the green folds of the mist-shrouded Magoebaskloof. This is a region of waterfalls and sparkling lakes, of deep pools and slippery streams, of gentle rolling hills and tea plantations. Eastwards, not far from the land of the legendary Rain Queen, Modjadji, and the primitive cycads that bear her name, the Great Letaba River winds through a countryside of wild flowers and fruit, known to early inhabitants as 'the happy land'.*

*In the far Northern Transvaal, where the Soutpansberg forms a natural east-west barricade across the land, dusty mountain tracks wind through forests of Cape chestnut and stinkwood, and romantic hiking trails traverse a hidden world of animals and birds. Beyond the Soutpansberg, the vegetation changes again. This is the beginning of the real Africa, where huge baobabs tower above a tropical parkland of rolling savannah and mopane trees; where the great north road bypasses nature reserves teeming with game, where the mighty Limpopo snakes along the northern frontier, separating the south from the endless wilderness of the African continent.*

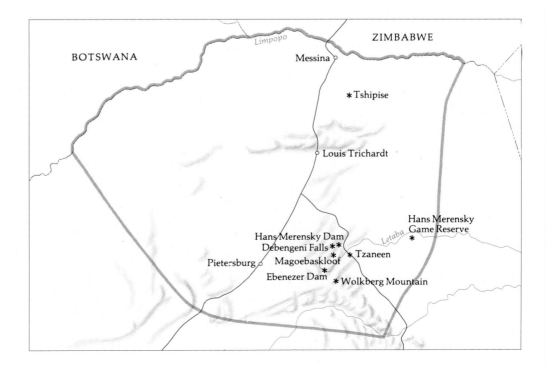

*Hippo and crocodile lurk beneath the lazy brown waters of the Letaba River, which snakes its way through the Hans Merensky Game Reserve.*

## CAVES OF HAUNTING SPLENDOUR

*A vertical shaft, discovered accidentally by a farmer's son on the slopes of the Wolkberg, south of Magoebaskloof in 1927, leads into one of the most spectacular sequences of underground chambers in the world. Known today as the Wolkberg Caves, this sequence is a subterranean wonderland of placid lakes, surrounded by towering statues of stalactites and stalagmites. Illuminated, these dripstone giants turn the monumental caverns into eerie arenas of ghost-like forms.*

*Born in the mists of the Wolkberg Mountains southwest of Tzaneen, a surging stream plummets over a precipice into a deep gorge below.*

*Ripples accentuate a river bed's contours near Debengeni Falls.*

*Cascading waters of the Debengeni Falls, flanked by the tumbling greenery of c riverine forest, plunge into a tranquil pool.*

*The lush, forested hills of the lower Mabitse valley loom over the placid waters of the Hans Merensky Dam near Duiwelskloof.*

*The cool waters of the Hans Merensky Dam shimmer in the sun. Pine and eucalyptus forests cover the surrounding mountains.*

*Forested banks and cloudy skies stare at their reflections in rivers and dams teeming with fish near Tzaneen in the northeastern Transvaal.*

## TOWERING MONARCH OF THE NORTH

*Legend has it in Africa that the mighty baobab tree, because of its enormous size, is dumped upon the earth from the heavens. In fact, the baby baobab is so different in appearance to its parents that even the San believed that these trees did not grow — they just arrived. With a lifespan of up to 1000 years, and an average diameter of about seven metres, the baobab is the undisputed monarch of trees and plants, dominating the savannah of the northern Transvaal with its huge bulbous trunk, and root-like branches clawing the sky.*

*Mopane trees dressed in the rich, golden plumage of autumn.*

*Imposing colossus of the bushveld, this giant baobab tree near Tshipise in the far northern Transvaal towers above its kingdom.*

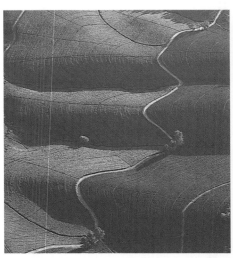

*Roller-coasting Magoebaskloof country.*

*Tea plantations plummet into forest-covered gorges in Magoebaskloof. This region is alive with the colours of subtropical flowers and fruits.*

*Indigenous mountain forest blankets the Magoebaskloof in contrasting shades of green. Monkeys, bushbuck and wild pigs live here.*

*The serenely beautiful waters of Ebenezer Dam form sinuous curves in a landscape which is dominated by mountains and rolling forests.*

*Hills, covered with forests of eucalyptus and pine, slope gently down to the water's edge at the Ebenezer Dam in the northern Transvaal.*

*This prince of the plains takes a nap in the Kalahari Gemsbok National Park. As an adult lion, he will kill about 47 animals a year.*

*Nature provides a perfect camouflage for a hungry lioness as she waits for prey in long grass in the Kalahari Desert.*

*Alert and aloof, a cheetah keeps a watch on passing game in the Kalahari Gemsbok National Park. A cheetah's favourite prey is springbok.*

*A pair of lions slake their thirst at a water hole in the Kalahari Gemsbok National Park. Lions do most of their hunting at night.*

# A JOURNEY INTO THE HEART OF AFRICA

*T*HE EASTERN TRANSVAAL *is the cradle of the primeval spirit of Africa, a wilderness of grassy plains and mountains that plunges down precipitously from the Highveld plateau to the subtropical parkland of the Lowveld. Bisecting these two regions is the immense escarpment of the Drakensberg, whose ragged flanks tower above canyons and gorges of breathtaking beauty.*

*At the foothills of this mountainous backbone, and between its soaring peaks, are wooded valleys, caves and waterfalls, unforgettable lakes and dams; lichen-coloured cliffs and mountain passes that descend into the untamed bushveld. This is the Africa of Rider Haggard and Sir Percy FitzPatrick, where songs of adventure and romance were sung by ivory hunters and pioneers in the shadows of the bushwillow and baobab; where greedy prospectors scrambled for gold, leaving behind them deserted mines and ghost towns, and old places with historic names, such as Pilgrim's Rest, Bourke's Luck and Barberton.*

*Here, in this world of tangled bush and thorn trees, stretching from the Limpopo River in the north to the Crocodile River in the south, and to the feet of the Lebombo Mountains in the east, is one of the great natural sanctuaries of the world, the Kruger National Park. This is big-game country, where lion, leopard and cheetah pick and choose their prey from tens of thousands of antelope that roam the plains.*

*A mantle of pale-green grassland and dense bush covers the graceful slopes of these mountains near the old prospectors' town of Barberton.*

*Pine trees shrouded in mist near Graskop.*

*Slender trunks, suffused with the soft light of early morning, cast long shadows on the forest floor in a Mac-Mac pine plantation.*

*The Long Tom Pass between Lydenburg and Sabie traverses the magnificent, forested mountains of the Transvaal Drakensberg.*

*The Olifants River follows a spectacular course through bush-covered mountains near the Abel Erasmus Pass in the eastern Transvaal.*

## MAGICAL JOURNEY THROUGH THE 'BERG

*Precipitous gorges, deep valleys and sun-bronzed cliffs flank the road which winds through the Abel Erasmus Pass, west of the Blyde River Canyon. Climbing some 365 metres over the bush-covered slopes of the Transvaal Drakensberg from Ohrigstad, the pass then descends through sweeping valleys, dotted with rustic settlements. En route are spectacular views of the Olifants River Valley and the eastern Transvaal Lowveld. The pass was originally used by wagons travelling through the Drakensberg from the north.*

*A rocky promontory soars above the Abel Erasmus Pass.*

*Rugged giants of the Drakensberg, their faces streaked by erosion, overlook a wilderness of startling beauty near the Abel Erasmus Pass.*

*Their flame-red turrets pointing skywards, these aloes set the countryside ablaze with colour near Graskop in the eastern Transvaal.*

*Lichen drapes a tree near Mac-Mac Falls.*

*Rearing majestically out of a mountain forest, Pinnacle Rock commands sweeping views of the eastern Transvaal Lowveld near Graskop.*

## A SPARKLING THREAD IN A LAND OF GIANTS

*The Blyde (Joy) River, starting as a tiny silver thread beneath the ancient granite domes of the Transvaal Drakensberg, slashes its way through a landscape of brooding grandeur, bypassing old prospectors' posts, isolated forest stations and lichen-covered cliffs.*

*After its confluence with the Treur at Bourke's Luck, the river dives into a huge canyon, snaking its way along the bottom some 800 metres below the escarpment. Soaring above the Blyde River are the triplet peaks of the Three Rondavels and the huge, table-topped summit of Mariepskop — once the scene of savage conflicts between the Swazi, Pedi and Pulana people.*

*The canyon is a natural botanical garden where tree ferns, cycads, creepers and wild fig trees flourish in the company of proteas, orchids and ericas.*

*The placid waters of the Blydepoort Dam and the ancient buttresses of the Drakensberg create a landscape of enduring beauty.*

*Dark ravines and mountains tower above twisting valleys in the Blyde River Canyon.*

*An aura of timeless majesty radiates from the brooding peaks of the Three Rondavels, high above the valleys of the Blyde River Canyon.*

*Sheer cliffs and spectacular rock formations tower above churning waters at Bourke's Luck, where the Blyde and Treur rivers meet.*

*Nature sculpts her own flowerpots in rock near Bourke's Luck.*

## NATURE'S MASTERPIECE IN ROCK

*Spinning rocks and pebbles, flung around for thousands of years by swirling waters at the confluence of the Blyde and Treur rivers, have gouged out the spectacular formations that are known today as Bourke's Luck Potholes. The potholes, which began as shallow depressions, now have an average depth of two to three metres, although some of the oldest are over six metres deep. Thomas Bourke, who once owned the farm where this feature appears, discovered gold at the bottom of the holes. His farm became known as Bourke's Luck.*

*The continual grinding action of water-borne pebbles and sand has gouged these bizarre shapes out of rock at Bourke's Luck Potholes.*

*Cascading sheets of water, like these at Forest Falls, bring roaring symphonies of sound to the mountains of the Transvaal Drakensberg.*

*At Lisbon Falls, near Graskop, snow-white jets of water hurtle headlong over green-cloaked cliffs into a deep, sparkling pool.*

## SOUTHERN AFRICA'S TRUE HAVEN OF THE WILD

*Majestic in its vastness, inestimably rich in its teeming game, the Kruger National Park is a rolling expanse of savannah and bushveld, stretching 350 km from the Limpopo River in the north to the Crocodile River in the south. Undoubtedly one of the world's greatest game sanctuaries, the park accommodates at least 137 species of mammal, numbering more than 250 000, and several hundred bird, reptile, fish, amphibian and butterfly species of contrasting shapes and colours.*

*In addition, 300 species of tree thrive in the park's five main botanical divisions. This spectacular variety includes aromatic mopane trees, whose leaves are relished by antelope and elephant; acacia and bushwillow; and sycamore figs, marulas and flowering white pear trees.*

*The Limpopo comes down in flood in the Kruger National Park. The river forms a natural boundary between South Africa and Zimbabwe.*

*A great white egret skims above a river in the Kruger Park.*

*Hippo, their heads barely visible in the sombre light of the dying day, wallow in the swirling waters of the Sabie River near Skukuza.*

## GRASSLANDS OF SWAZILAND

*White rhino, hippo, giraffe, eland and
a variety of other wild animals roam
the beautiful grasslands of the
Mlilwane Wildlife Sanctuary in
Swaziland. Lying across the
escarpment that divides Swaziland's
highveld and lowveld, Mlilwane is a
refuge and breeding ground for more
than 240 different species of bird, from
blue crane to multicoloured sunbird.
Forming a natural backdrop to the
perennial streams, pools and vleis of
Mlilwane are the twin, sharp-peaked
koppies known as Sheba's Breasts.*

*The sugar cane fields of Swaziland cover the countryside with a rich, green blanket.*

*The waters of the Little Usutu River, fringed by dense bush and forests, plunge gracefully over the Mantenga Falls in Swaziland.*

*Rocky mountains form a natural backdrop to sloping grassland and pine forests in Swaziland's popular Mlilwane Wildlife Sanctuary.*

*The sun-splashed plains and thorny thickets of southern Africa are the home and final refuge of the world's most diverse and richest communities of wildlife. From rambling tusker to pygmy shrew, from fleet-footed antelope to loping giraffe, from orange-breasted sunbird to black-collared barbet, lives an astonishing family of mammals, reptiles, insects and birds — guided miraculously through the tumultuous passage of time by their overwhelming instinct for survival. Here, in the wild corners of southern Africa, where the primeval secrets of evolution have unfolded over the millennia, is the ultimate proof of the wonders of creation.*

*Tuned into danger, a group of impala stands watchfully in a thicket. These prancers of the wild can leap three metres into the air.*

*Surveillance is the key to survival for this alert female kudu in the Kruger National Park.*

*Waterbuck pause cautiously on the fringes of thick bush. These animals never stray far from a waterhole — hence their name.*

*Trunks outstretched, a herd of African elephants slake their thirst at a waterhole. Each adult consumes about 200 litres of water a day.*

*The neck of this graceful giraffe rises like a mottled periscope from the long grass of the Krugersdorp Game Reserve.*

# ENDLESS PLAINS ANOINTED IN GOLD

*HERE ARE THE ROLLING PRAIRIELANDS of southern Africa; a countryside of clean air, vast horizons and majestic sandstone mountains — a natural game park that has become the granary of the subcontinent. Perched on the high regions of South Africa's central plateau, and bounded in the north and south by the Vaal and Orange rivers, this is a land where rivers and mountains, grainlands and grasslands, and even the soil, have been struck with the colours of gold. Here the gently undulating plains are broken only by the graceful turrets of sandstone monoliths towering over rustic farmsteads and lazy rivers; where the sound of the wind whistling across the plains is interrupted by the murmurs and groans of weary windmills.*

*From the Orange River to the tawny coloured Vaal, through golden fields of wheat, maize and sunflowers, the Golden Way bisects a land of buried treasure — where vast resources of gold, pyrites and uranium lie concealed in sediments which were laid down through geologic upheavals between 125 and 250 million years ago.*

*Towards the east, lush green grasslands between the Rooiberg and the foothills of the Maluti Mountains carpet the way to the magnificent scenery of the Golden Gate Highlands National Park. Here, through the erosive forces of wind and water on the crumbly surface of the Clarens sandstone, nature has modelled a spectacular, multicoloured landscape, forming hollow valleys with sparkling streams, gouging out deep caves on flat-topped mountains, forming totem poles of balancing rock and providing vantage points with endless views.*

*A waterbed for autumn leaves.*

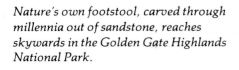

*Nature's own footstool, carved through millennia out of sandstone, reaches skywards in the Golden Gate Highlands National Park.*

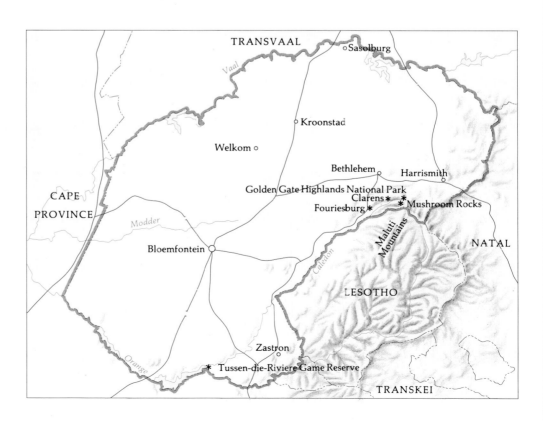

*Sandstone buttresses, washed by the sun, cast eerie shadows over the beautiful, rolling valleys of the eastern Orange Free State.*

*Sandstone hills rear up like lonely sentinels across a landscape of undulating green near Fouriesburg in the eastern Orange Free State.*

## THE CHANGING FACE OF SANDSTONE

*The Clarens sandstone of the eastern Orange Free State is one
of the most stunning of all geologic formations. Formerly
referred to as Cave sandstone, for the deep caves in its cliffs,
this sandstone was laid down millions of years ago on top of the
fossil-bearing Molteno Beds and Red Beds. Suffused with iron
oxides, the individual grains have become transmitters of the
brilliant colours which caress the hills and valleys of the eastern
Free State.*

*Fertile fields of wheat and maize bring a bounteous harvest to Free State farms nestling in the lap of Lesotho's Maluti Mountains.*

*The foothills of the Drakensberg in the Orange Free State provide an awesome spectacle of vast plateaux, rugged peaks and precipitous gorges.*

*A bush-covered mountain, its flanks bearing deep furrows of erosion, towers above the hinterland on South Africa's great central plateau.*

*The pinnacles of distant mountains pierce the pale-blue sky in the eastern Orange Free State, a paradise for nature lovers and hikers.*

*Farmlands create a fairytale setting near the hamlet of Clarens.*

## THE ENCHANTED VALLEY

*The fertile valley of the Little Caledon River which sweeps its way through the rolling countryside of the eastern Orange Free State, is a spectacular example of water's erosive effect on sandstone. Here the river has worn down age-old deposits of Clarens sandstone, creating a wonderland of rigid shapes and forms. Most impressive of all is the Golden Gate itself, the sandstone cliff which looms above the right-hand bank of the Little Caledon near its headwaters. These sandstone giants along the course of the Little Caledon, covered by carpets of lush, green grass, and surrounded by golden fields of wheat and maize create a landscape of unforgettable beauty, highlighted by the colours of flowers such as arum lilies, red-hot pokers, fire lilies and watsonias.*

*The bushy grasslands of Tussen-die-Riviere game farm, wedged between the Orange and Caledon rivers in the southern Free State.*

## A GOLDEN GATE BECKONING ALL

*The radiant sandstone cliffs, the
sweeping valleys and the shimmering
waters of the Golden Gate Highlands
National Park have lured man and
animals to the Little Caledon river
valley since prehistoric times.
Mammal-like reptiles, Stone-age man,
San hunters and teeming herds of game
have walked in the shadows of the gold
and copper cliffs, sculpted through the
ages by the erosive forces of wind and
rain. Further down the time scale,
modern man has sought refuge and
peace in the lee of these graceful giants,
reflecting on their brilliant colours and
many changing moods.*

*Emerald hills tumble into tranquil valleys at the Golden Gate Highlands National Park.*

*Water and sky merge in a startling symphony of blue under the lustrous, ever-changing faces of these sandstone giants at Golden Gate.*

*The profile of a sandstone cliff, rugged and scarred by erosion through the ages, looms prominently above a watered valley at Golden Gate.*

*Whitewashed ridges of Clarens sandstone slash through valleys of gold and green in the eastern Free State's mountainous amphitheatre.*

*The contours of newly ploughed fields in the eastern Orange Free State create symmetrical patterns on the sun-soaked countryside.*

*Tantalising blooms of cosmos bring a kaleidoscope of colour to the undulating grasslands of the Golden Gate Highlands National Park.*

*Splashed by the sun, the mighty flanks of Mushroom Rocks rear out of the shadows of the Golden Gate Highlands National Park.*

Tireless builders of the land, the bountiful grasses of southern Africa serve as a vital source of food for countless living creatures; their roots act as a bulwark against wind and soil erosion; their stalks as a hiding place for insects and birds. Grasses add form and colour to the earth, inviting life to wilderness and wasteland. Languid in their movements, exquisite in their forms, they are the universal evocation of the wonder of living things.

*Golden stalks of Kalahari grass dance in the wind of dawn.*

*The long grasses of the northern Cape's savannah plains surround these early grazers with contrasting shades of beige and brown.*

*Like silent sentinels at the gates of dawn, a regiment of stalks stands motionless and proud on the floor of the Kalahari Desert.*

*Crowned by the rays of the setting sun, these clumps of dune grass stand aloof as a patina of changing hues settles on the horizon.*

# ANCIENT KINGDOM IN THE CLOUDS

*L*IKE MAJESTIC TURRETS *ascending from a basalt castle, the peaks of Lesotho tower above a highland of astonishing beauty. Here is the Switzerland of southern Africa, a fairytale kingdom in the sky, geologically restructured more than 150 million years ago, when a large-scale eruption broke through the yellow-red sandstone surface, depositing on top of it a volcanic slab nearly 1500 metres thick. Since then, erosion has eaten away at the crumbly basalt surface, creating a masterpiece of tumbling mountains, verdant kloofs and table-top plateaux, extending 250 km from north to south.*

*From the golden wheatfields of the western lowlands to the craggy peaks of Thabana Ntlenyana, southern Africa's highest mountain in the east, Lesotho is a natural amphitheatre, embracing some of the most spectacular scenery in southern Africa. Balancing rocks, waterfalls, deep gorges, pinnacles and spires, mountain springs gushing with sparkling water, homely huts and chalets nestling in the mountains — these are some of the delights that have enticed nature lovers worldwide.*

*The seasons cast their own spell over the land: hillsides, splashed with the pinks and lilac colours of spring, are blanketed with snow in winter; deep summer pools and trout-filled streams ice up, and an eerie silence descends over the high regions.*

*Adding eloquence to the primeval beauty of Lesotho are remarkable fossil footprints left by reptiles that stalked the region 200 million years ago, rich galleries of San paintings colouring the walls of caves in the foothills of the Maluti Mountains and the haunting, flat-topped 'Mountain of the night', Thaba Bosiu.*

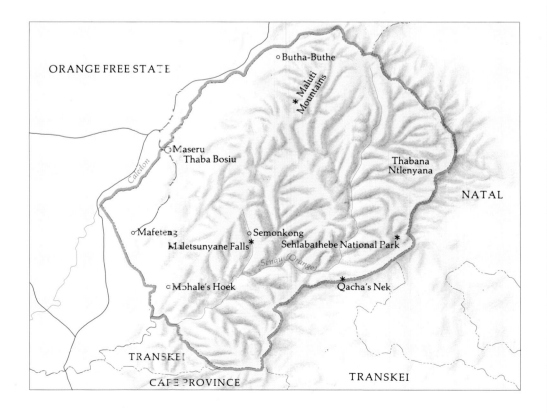

*Golden fields of wheat, maize and sorghum cover the lowlands of Lesotho in winter. Less than 12 per cent of this mountain kingdom is arable.*

*Craggy mountains dominate this tranquil landscape in the Sehlabathebe National Park.*

*Covered by a canopy of rolling grasslands, the slopes of these mountains in central Lesotho fall gently to the valley floor.*

*A rugged mountainside forms an imposing backdrop to fertile grainlands in northwestern Lesotho, once the home of dinosaurs.*

## NATURE'S OWN MASTERPIECE IN ROCK

*A ragged roof of basalt mountains dominates Lesotho. Seen
from the air, this roof is a corrugated landscape of crisscrossing
mountain chains and deeply etched valleys and gorges. Erosion
over millions of years has sculpted a geologic masterpiece in the
stratified rock, exposing the alternating colours of even the
very lowest layers. From hard sandstones to friable shales and
mudstones, these horizontal layers underlying the basalt peaks
colour the mountain kingdom with contrasting shades of
purple and red, grey and white, orange and pink.*

*Soaring peaks thrust through banks of cloud at Qacha's Nek.*

*The corrugated mountains, deep valleys and precipitous gorges of central Lesotho testify to millions of years of soil erosion.*

*Late afternoon sun gives an ashen complexion to the peaks of the Maluti Mountains. These mountains are over 150 million years old.*

*A silver thread running through a landscape of giants  the Maletsunyane River has excavated a deep gorge in the Maluti Mountains.*

*A torrent of thundering water plummets 193 metres over a basalt rim at Maletsunyane Falls, one of the highest waterfalls in Africa.*

Bearer of light to the dark places of the subcontinent, the moon acts as a great celestial magnet on the seas that wash the shores of southern Africa, affecting the lives of billions of organisms large and small. With its endless elliptical orbit around the earth, the moon has stirred the passions and wonder of all mankind, from ancestral Nguni and Kalahari San, to space-age astronauts tottering along its crusty face.

*The moon casts its mystical light upon the Indian Ocean off Natal.*

*In its gracious orbit around the earth, the pale moon illuminates the evening sky above Punda Maria in the Kruger National Park.*

*The moon setting over the ochre dunes of the Kalahari creates a startling contrast of colours. Like the earth, it rotates on its own axis.*

# THROUGH THE DUNE FRONTIER

*T*HE SAN HUNTERS *called it 'the land God made in anger' —
an endless sea of sun-bronzed desert dunes and rocky plains
bisected by primordial mountain chains and dried-out river beds.
Seafarers, hurled with their ships upon the wasteland of the Namib,
called it the Skeleton Coast; the hinterland, a place of desolation.*

*To all who have crossed her borders, Namibia is an enigma —
unrelentingly harsh, but also breathtakingly beautiful. From the desert
in the west, to the arid plains of the Kalahari in the east; from the
savannah grasslands of the north, to the Fish River Canyon in the
south, the countryside is locked in a perpetual battle against drought.*

*The savage seesaw of life and death in Namibia is no more apparent
than in the Etosha Pan, where the tempo of life and the migrations of
massive herds are mapped out by the rain and sun. In the dry season,
the sun-baked, salt-encrusted pan is a place of dust devils and mirages,
where the earth cracks in the scorching heat. Then torrential rains bring
new life to the land, and a green lawn of grass covers the countryside.*

*The rest of Namibia continues to ache in the sun. At Sossusvlei, the
wind brings little relief as it sculpts amazing shapes out of bronzed dune
giants; up in the plains of the Marienfluss, animals seek cover from the
sun under sunburnt rocks; and on dry river beds across the gravel
plains, remote communities of man dig deep for water.*

*Furrows wrinkle the face of the Namib.*

*A phalanx of rocks halts the golden sands
of the Namib near the Sesriem Canyon.
Vast plains spread westward.*

*The lion-coloured grasslands of Namibia merge with mountains on the distant horizon under a sheet of summer rain clouds.*

*An eerie glow of golden-green descends on the grasslands and mountains near Sesriem at the end of another blistering day.*

*At Sossusvlei, nature moulds her own masterpieces in the slipfaces, ridges and hollows of some of the highest sand dunes in the world.*

*Periodic floods have halted the march of these enormous dunes along the banks of the Kuiseb River in the Namib-Naukluft Park.*

*Rocks dating back millions of years bisect the tufted grasslands of Namibia.*

*Flanked by avenues of trees, the dry bed of the Kuiseb River heads seawards. The river demarcates the Namib's dune sea and gravel plains.*

*Honed by the southwest winds of the Namib, longitudinal dune chains form spectacular ripples along the banks of the Kuiseb River.*

*A masterpiece in sand — a crescent-shaped dune, or barchan.*

## THE REMARKABLE DUNES OF THE NAMIB

*An unbroken sea of huge, longitudinal dune chains, 500 km long and up to 100 km wide, is concentrated in the Namib Desert between Walvis Bay and Luderitz. Soaring up to 250 metres in height, and buffeted by southwest and east winds, the crests of these dunes have been fashioned into repetitive S-shapes, rising and falling to form a chain of summits. White-to-yellow in colour near the coast, the dunes become bronzed-to-red further inland — the result of oxidation.*

*Ancient mountains congregate around the canyons of the Swakop and Khan rivers, revealing a kaleidoscope of eroded sediments.*

*The sighing winds of the Namib whip tons of sand from the crests of these shifting dunes. The Nama call these winds 'Soo-oop-wa'.*

*Wind is the great sculptor of the Namib's dune sea, continually altering, remodelling and replacing the awesome linear forms.*

*Soothing mists from the sea roll in over the Namib's dunes one day in five, bringing vital sustenance to the desert's fauna and flora.*

*A highway of sand runs between the deep-blue waters of the Atlantic and the dunes of the Namib Desert on the west coast of Namibia.*

*The bone-bleaching dunes of the Namib taper off gradually to meet the sea along the desolate shoreline of the Skeleton Coast.*

## DESOLATION ON THE COAST OF DEATH

*Littered with the bones of ships and men, the Skeleton Coast
stretches from the Kunene River in the north to Cape Cross in
the south — a desolate and treacherous coastal terrace that has
no equal on earth. A graveyard of sand, an inhospitable
wasteland; an endless source of inspiration for legends of woe
— the Skeleton Coast has all these attributes. But more than
this, it is also a place of enduring tranquillity, where the wind
plays games with the sand, and rolling fog brings regeneration
and life to the thirsty land within. Forty kilometres wide,
interminably long, the Skeleton Coast is a wilderness of white
sands and wide horizons where a diverse and hardy world of
living things does battle with the elements in one of the world's
harshest environments.*

*The dark waters of Lake Cponono carve patterns beautiful and bizarre out of the sprawling plains of southern Owamboland.*

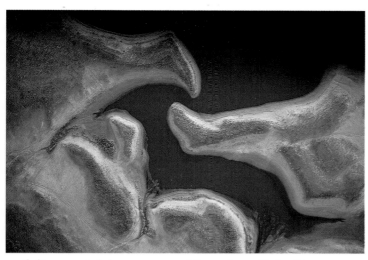

*Salt-encrusted shores surround the waters of Lake Oponono.*

*Dwarfed from the air and camouflaged by cloud, the mighty Orange River meanders seaward to form Namibia's southern boundary.*

## THE RIVER THAT DANCES THROUGH THE DESERT

*The mighty Kunene is a river of changing moods and character. Exiting Angola as a wide, sluggish waterway, it enters Namibia in a spectacular 100-metre cascade at the Ruacana Falls. Passing the Zebra Mountains, the river gains momentum, sweeping past numerous islands in a shou of dancing, sparkling white water, until at the Epupa Falls, it plunges into a fissure 40 metres deep.*

*Metamorphosed by the changing landscape, the Kunene starts tumbling through precipitous mountain gorges, eventually entering the majestic 70-km long Marienfluss plains. Between Marienfluss and the coast, the river slashes its way through granite cliffs and towering sand dunes, until, seemingly exhausted by the rigours of its journey, it tapers off as a brackish lagoon on the edge of the sea.*

*Alternating stripes on the Zebra Mountains in Kaokoland.*

*The fingers of the Kunene River grope their way through remote mountains which flank the sandy expanse of the Marienfluss plains.*

*Like an intricate root system, the dry river bed and its tributaries stretch out across the parched scrubland of central Kaokoland.*

*Dry river beds snake like barren arteries across central Kaokoland. Wild animals follow these corridors in search of food and water.*

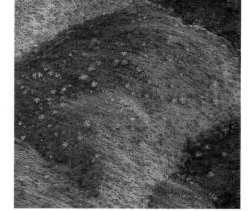

*Craters on the Baynes Mountains.*

*The Kunene River cuts a narrow path through mountains in northern Kaokoland.*

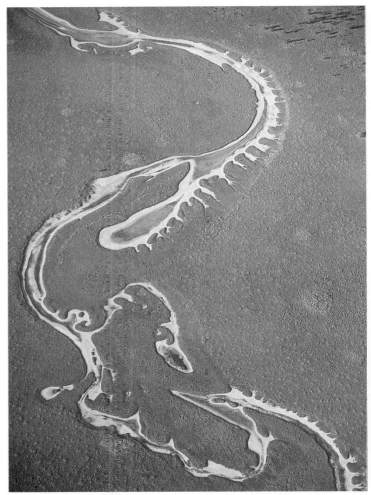

## ETOSHA — PLACE OF THE SHIMMERING SUN

*The Etosha Pan, cursed by drought and lashed by the sun for eight months a year, becomes an enormous, shallow lake, sparkling with life, when the floodwaters of the Ekuma and Omuramba Ovambo rivers drain into it from the north during the rainy season.*

*New grasses emerge, the land changes colour, micro-organisms flourish, and thousands of greater and lesser flamingoes descend on the pan to breed. Joining them are an enormous number of waterbirds, ranging from Egyptian geese and egrets, to yellow-billed storks and herons. Throughout the pan, wildlife abounds; kudu and zebra, springbok and impala, wildebeest and red hartebeest move from one flush of newly sprung grass to another, while lion and cheetah follow the herds, looking for easy prey.*

*The salt-saturated Ekuma River snakes its way through Etosha.*

*Floor of the Etosha Pan — a sterile, saline desert plain. When good rains fall, one-metre deep sheets of shallow water cover the pan.*

*Driven on by their ruthless instinct for survival, animal herds follow an intricate complex of game trails across the Etosha Pan.*

*Rain transforms a hostile wasteland into a life-giving oasis in the Etosha National Park — one of the greatest game parks in Africa.*

*Dense bush gives way to large open plains in the Etosha National Park, where mighty herds range free of the ravages of man.*

*Sucked dry by suffocating winds and parched by the relentless sun, a cracked pan reveals the vast desolation of the Namib Desert.*

*The Namib's face bakes in the sun.*

The western and central plains of southern Africa were known to the early Khoikhoi as the 'place of great dryness' — a parched, arid expanse of semidesert and scrubland, scourged for millennia by the relentless rays of the sun. Today, the legend of the Khoikhoi lives on, as pitiless droughts continue to wring the lifeblood from animals and the land.

In the Kalahari and the Great Karoo, pans dry up overnight and the surface of the soil cracks under the searing heat. In the Namib Desert, insects and animals burrow under the baking sand, searching for relief from boiling temperatures. In the eastern, central and northern Cape, cattle and sheep grow hungry and gaunt as their waterholes vanish under cloudless skies. Crops wither, some farmers despair. This is the toll taken by drought in a land where water is sometimes rarer than gold.

*Drought sculpts a grotesque jigsaw puzzle on the floor of the Namib, described once as an 'infernal region of frightful desolation'.*

# PHOTO CREDITS

Picture credits for each page read from top to bottom, using the top of the picture as the reference point. Where the tops of two or more pictures are on the same level, credits read from left to right.

4 Trevor Barrett
7 Anthony Bannister
8 Walter Knirr
9 Ken Gerhardt/Photo Access
10 Both David Steele/Photo Access
11 Jean Morris
12 Anthony Bannister
13 Herman Potgieter, Gordon Douglas
14 Ken Gerhardt/Photo Access
15 Ken Gerhardt/Photo Access
16 Herman Potgieter,
   Anthony Bannister
17 Anthony Bannister
18 Peter Pickford
19 Peter Steyn/Photo Access,
   Ken Gerhardt/Photo Access
20 Zane Erasmus/Photo Access,
   David Steele/Photo Access
21 Herman Potgieter
22 Val Johnstone/Photo Access,
   Herman Potgieter
23 Herman Potgieter
24 Jean Morris, Mark van Aardt
25 Wolfgang Ochojski/Photo Access,
   Jean Morris
26 Gerald Cubitt
27 Zane Erasmus/Photo Access,
   Peter John
28 Herman Potgieter
29 David Steele/Photo Access
30 Ken Gerhardt/Photo Access
31 John Paisley/Photo Access,
   Herman Potgieter
32 Gerald Cubitt
33 Peter John, Gordon Douglas
34 David Steele/Photo Access
35 Both Anthony Bannister
36 Both Anthony Bannister
37 Anthony Bannister
38 All Anthony Bannister
39 Anthony Bannister
40 Mark van Aardt
41 Anthony Bannister
42 Anthony Bannister
43 Francois Le Roux/Photo Access
44 Anthony Bannister
45 Anthony Bannister
46 Gordon Douglas
47 David Steele/Photo Access
48 David Steele/Photo Access,
   Herman Potgieter
49 David Steele/Photo Access
50 Herman Potgieter
51 Anthony Bannister, Peter John
52 Gerald Cubitt
53 Jean Morris, David Steele/
   Photo Access
54 Herman Potgieter
55 Jean Morris
56 Anthony Bannister, Gerald Cubitt
57 Anthony Bannister
58 Jean Morris
59 David Steele/Photo Access,
   Herman Potgieter
60 Herman Potgieter

61 Both Herman Potgieter
62 All Anthony Bannister
63 Anthony Bannister, David Steele/
   Photo Access, Anthony Bannister,
   David Steele/Photo Access
64 Anthony Bannister
65 David Steele/Photo Access
66 David Steele/Photo Access
67 Walter Knirr
68 Gerald Cubitt, John Paisley/
   Photo Access
69 Anthony Bannister
70 Walter Knirr
71 David Steele/Photo Access
72 Both David Steele/Photo Access
73 Walter Knirr
74 Gerald Cubitt
75 Mark van Aardt
76 Gerald Cubitt
77 Both Herman Potgieter
78 David Steele/Photo Access,
   Anthony Bannister
79 Walter Knirr
80 Both Anthony Bannister
81 Anthony Bannister
82 Both Anthony Bannister
83 Anthony Bannister
84 Anthony Bannister, David Steele/
   Photo Access
85 David Steele/Photo Access
86 Both David Steele/Photo Access
87 Anthony Bannister, David Steele/
   Photo Access, David Steele/
   Photo Access
88 Jean Morris, David Steele/
   Photo Access, Jean Morris
89 Jean Morris, David Steele/
   Photo Access
90 Gerald Cubitt
92 Both David Steele/Photo Access
93 Both David Steele/Photo Access
94 David Steele/Photo Access
95 David Steele/Photo Access
96 David Steele/Photo Access
97 Both David Steele/Photo Access
98 Herman Potgieter
99 John Paisley/Photo Access
100 Both Herman Potgieter
101 Herman Potgieter
102 Herman Potgieter
103 Gerald Cubitt
104 Gordon Douglas
105 Mark van Aardt
106 David Steele/Photo Access
   Peter John
107 Gerald Cubitt, Walter Knirr
108 Anthony Bannister
109 David Steele/Photo Access
110 Gerald Cubitt
111 Peter John, Herman Potgieter
112 Gerald Cubitt
113 Gerald Cubitt
114 Peter Pickford
115 Anthony Bannister, David
   Steele/Photo Access
116 Both David Steele/Photo Access
117 All David Steele/Photo Access
118 Walter Knirr
120 Peter John, Jean Morris
121 Gordon Douglas
122 Gerald Cubitt

123 Walter Knirr
124 Herman Potgieter
125 Gerald Cubitt, Walter Knirr
126 Walter Knirr
127 Herman Potgieter, Walter Knirr
128 Herman Potgieter
129 Walter Knirr
130 Gordon Douglas,
131 Herman Potgieter
132 Gordon Douglas,
   David Steele/Photo Access
133 Gerald Cubitt
134 Gordon Douglas
135 Walter Knirr
136 Walter Knirr
137 Walter Knirr
138 Jean Morris
139 Both Jean Morris
140 Peter John
141 Herman Potgieter, John Paisley/
   Photo Access
142 Jean Morris, Anthony Bannister
143 Jean Morris
144 Walter Knirr
145 Anthony Bannister
146 Anthony Bannister,
   David Steele/Photo Access
147 David Steele/Photo Access
148 Both Anthony Bannister
149 David Steele/Photo Access
150 Both Gerhardus du Plessis/
   Photo Access
151 Gerhardus du Plessis/Photo Access
152 Jean Morris
154 Mark van Aardt
155 Gerald Cubitt
156 Walter Knirr
157 Walter Knirr
158 Gerald Cubitt
159 Gerald Cubitt, Anthony Bannister
160 Walter Knirr
161 Walter Knirr
162 Both Anthony Bannister
163 Walter Knirr
164 Both Herman Potgieter
165 Walter Knirr
166 Peter John, Peter Pickford
167 Peter Pickford
168 Gerald Cubitt
170 Gerald Cubitt
171 John Paisley/Photo Access,
   Walter Knirr
172 Gordon Douglas
173 Walter Knirr
174 Walter Knirr
175 Both Mark van Aardt
176 Both Herman Potgieter
177 Gerald Cubitt
178 Herman Potgieter
179 Walter Knirr
180 Anthony Bannister
181 Anthony Bannister
182 Anthony Bannister
183 Anthony Bannister
184 David Steele/Photo Access
185 Gerhardus du Plessis/Photo Access
186 David Steele/Photo Access
187 Gordon Douglas
188 Walter Knirr
189 Jean Morris, Herman Potgieter
190 Walter Knirr

191 Mark van Aardt, Walter Knirr
192 David Steele/Photo Access
193 Both Walter Knirr
194 David Steele/Photo Access
195 Anthony Bannister, Walter Knirr
196 Walter Knirr
197 Walter Knirr
198 Anthony Bannister
199 Anthony Bannister,
   David Steele/Photo Access
200 John Paisley/Photo Access,
   David Steele/Photo Access
201 Gerald Cubitt
202 Anthony Bannister
203 Anthony Bannister,
   David Steele/Photo Access
204 Anthony Bannister
205 Anthony Bannister
206 Walter Knirr
207 Anthony Bannister
208 Walter Knirr
209 David Steele/Photo Access
210 Gordon Douglas
211 Gerald Cubitt
212 Both Herman Potgieter
213 Gordon Douglas,
   Anthony Bannister
214 Clarke Gittens/Photo Access,
   Anthony Bannister
215 Fred Hodgson/Photo Access
216 Herman Potgieter
217 Herman Potgieter
218 Walter Knirr
219 Walter Knirr
220 Both Anthony Bannister
221 Anthony Bannister, Peter Pickford
222 Gordon Douglas
224 Gerald Cubitt, Gordon Douglas
225 Jean Morris
226 Both Gordon Douglas
227 Gordon Douglas
228 Gordon Douglas
229 Gordon Douglas
230 Anthony Bannister,
   David Steele/Photo Access
231 Anthony Bannister
232 Walter Knirr
233 Anthony Bannister
234 Ernst Rohe/Photo Access,
   Walter Knirr
235 Walter Knirr
236 Anthony Bannister
237 Both Ernst Rohe/Photo Access
238 Anthony Bannister
239 Both Anthony Bannister
240 Both Anthony Bannister
241 Anthony Bannister
242 Anthony Bannister
243 Anthony Bannister
244 Anthony Bannister
245 Both Anthony Bannister
246 Both Anthony Bannister
247 Anthony Bannister
248 Anthony Bannister
249 Both Anthony Bannister
250 Both Anthony Bannister
251 Anthony Bannister
252 Anthony Bannister
253 Anthony Bannister
254 Anthony Bannister
255 Anthony Bannister, Gerald Cubitt

Reproduction by Bright Arts (HK) Ltd. Printed and bound by C & C Joint Printing Co (HK) Ltd